GROWING AND SUSTAINING STUDENT-CENTERED SCIENCE CLASSROOMS

David Stroupe

HARVARD EDUCATION PRESS

Cambridge, Massachusetts

Paperback ISBN 978-1-68253-795-4

Library of Congress Cataloging-in-Publication Data is on file.

Published by Harvard Education Press,
an imprint of the Harvard Education Publishing Group

Harvard Education Press
8 Story Street
Cambridge, MA 02138

Cover Design: Ciano Design
Cover Image: SDI Productions/E+ via Getty Images

The typefaces in this book are Geller and Unitext.

*This book is dedicated to
teachers and students
who are doing the daily work
of building powerful and
equitable classroom communities.*

CONTENTS

Introduction   1

ONE   Confronting Epistemic Injustice   15

TWO   Pernicious Myths About Science and Teaching
      Classrooms That Limit Opportunities for Students   35

THREE Looking in the Mirror   51

FOUR Purposeful Talk Moves to Signal the Value of
      Students' Ideas, Experiences, and Communities   63

FIVE Making Knowledge Production Practices Visible
      and Shaped by Students   81

SIX   Tensions, Complexities, and Learning to See
      Opportunities   99

SEVEN Shared Goals for Schools and Communities   111

EIGHT Words of Wisdom from Anna and Lindsay   123

NINE Moving Forward   139

      Notes   147

      Acknowledgments   153

      About the Author   155

      Index   157

Introduction

TEACHING HAS ALWAYS been a crucial and underappreciated profession across the world. Almost everyone spends some time in a school, and in those spaces, teachers play an important role in designing and facilitating opportunities for participation and learning. Many people fondly remember a favorite teacher and classroom or, conversely, might hope to forget a school that made them feel rejected. While society might collectively forget, those of us who spend time in schools know that teachers and administrator have a great responsibility as we shape the lives of children. By representing and upholding equitable communities and participatory structures that ensure powerful learning opportunities for children, especially those from marginalized communities, teachers and administrators can help change the world. While easy to think and say, such short-term and long-term work is difficult to enact. Therefore, I want to help you spark conversations about how we can individually and collectively work together to reimagine your classroom and school as sites of equitable learning opportunities.

We will start our collective conversation and collaborative work around classroom and school communities by peeking into the classrooms of two teachers, who I will refer to as Teacher A and Teacher B. Both teachers graduated from the same teacher preparation program, and both taught life science in very diverse schools in the same district. However, Teacher A and Teacher B differed in how they chose to open up, or restrict, avenues for student talk and participation around knowledge in their science classrooms. Let's look at an example from each class, both of which occurred at the beginning of the school year. As teachers and administrators, we know that the beginning of the school year is such an important time for building a foundation for a science community. For each example, imagine you are sitting in the room, as I was when I watched these lessons unfold, and immerse yourself in the sights and sounds of middle and high school science classes.

In Teacher A's classroom, students are learning about why identical twins look alike, and why differences might exist even with their similar DNA. Following the first lessons in which students share some initial ideas about why identical twins might look similar and begin to hear terms such as "dominant," "recessive," "trait,", "allele," Teacher A decides that students should complete Punnett Squares to visualize how physical traits and alleles are related. If you need a quick refresher about Punnett Squares, recall that a Punnett Square provides a space for visualizing and writing potential allele combinations for one offspring given the parents' alleles. A typical example usually includes a two-by-two table, with two alleles from one parent on the side of the table, and two alleles from another parent above the table.

In this example, Teacher A demonstrated how to complete and interpret a Punnett Square and asked students, in groups of two or three, to attempt three example squares as practice. After showing students how to correctly complete the squares, Teacher A wrote a new square on the whiteboard for students to attempt individually. As the murmurs of talk receded into individual pondering of the problem, a quiet student—one I had never heard speak in class before this moment—raised his hand. Tentatively, he asked, "Excuse me, Ms. [A]? I have a question. When we do Punnett Squares, we also do examples with four kids. What if there are five kids? Where does the fifth kid go?"

Let's pause here, in this moment, to think about the layers of what the quiet student said. For some people, the focus might fall on science knowledge and the student's "incorrect" idea about Punnett Squares; after all, the cells in a Punnett Square provide a space for people to record possible allele combinations for an individual, and do not represent multiple children. Others might be interested in the student deciding to share a question in the class. What prompted this student to speak at this time, when they had never previously spoken in class? Another layer is that the student might be speaking on behalf of other students in the class. After all, if one student thinks that Punnett Squares illustrate multiple children, how many other students have the same question? While Teacher A could have been considering any of those possibilities, their thinking remained invisible as they said back to the student: "That's not how this works. We need to keep moving to finish the practice problems." While this talk move (a talk move is a statement made by a teacher or student to open up or restrict future classroom talk) may seem routine to some teacher and administrators, from the perspective of this student, Teacher A's words caused silence. Whenever I visited the classroom for the remainder of the school year, this student never spoke in class again—not to the teacher, other students, or administrators who entered the space.

Let's move from Teacher A's classroom to Teacher B's classroom, just few miles away. In Teacher B's classroom, students were learning about evolution by asking "How did we get chihuahuas from wolves?" which a student asked Teacher B in the hallway after school early in the academic year. Before the class began, Teacher B told me that they wanted to make students feel like their ideas had value, and that, like scientists, ideas about the world could be put into the public plane of talk and analyzed by a larger community. For this lesson, Teacher B created a poster using a large piece of construction paper and wrote a title: "Our hypotheses: From Wolf to Woof." After students had five minutes to discuss ideas in pairs, Teacher B announced that the whole class would now think together, given their discussions. To catalyze the conversation, Teacher B asked students to share ideas about why chihuahuas exist, especially if they look so different from wolves. Importantly, Teacher B told the class to share ideas, if possible, that they considered during conversations with peers. After several students offered hypotheses ("Maybe the DNA changed because of a mutation," "Maybe a wolf had pups that were all really different in size"), a series of student comments occurred in quick succession:

STUDENT 1: "Maybe mating with a rabbit would make a dog small."
STUDENT 2: "Yeah, a rabbit would make a small baby, not a Great Dane."

STUDENT 3 "What about the ankle biter? Maybe a wolf mated
with a rabbit to make an ankle biter." [The class started calling
chihuahuas "ankle biters" as a joke.]

Again, let's pause here to consider the layers of complexity that arise simultaneously when these students shared ideas. Some teachers and administrators might worry about the students' wrong ideas—we know that wolves and rabbits cannot create babies together. Other people might wonder about the students' purpose in sharing ideas: Were they seeking attention, or purposefully trying to disrupt the class? Still others might be focused on Teacher B's actions, questioning whether such a conversation is a productive use of class time.

Teacher B, however, recognized this moment as a point of departure from instruction that might limit students' opportunities to engage in knowledge practices in a classroom. Here's how the next minute of class unfolded:

TEACHER B: "Wait, why did you just joke that a rabbit mating with a
wolf would make an ankle-biter dog as opposed to a Great Dane?"
STUDENT 3: Maybe because ... rabbits are small. And ankle biters
are small.
STUDENT 2: Oh, you feel my word. [Student 2 originally injected "ankle
biter" into the science community.]
TEACHER B: It's become a class word now.
STUDENT 3: Right. Rabbits have big ears. And ankle biters have ears
that bend and look like rabbit ears.
TEACHER B: So what are you really suggesting about where chihuahuas
get their traits?
MULTIPLE STUDENTS IN CLASS CALL OUT: From their parents.

Once students chimed into the discussion, the classroom talk exploded. Almost every student in the class raised their hand to contribute to the conversation, and by the end of class, three important ideas emerged: (1) parents must be close together to make babies (but all parents or just some species?, several students wondered); (2) babies get traits from parents; (3) not all babies are identical to parents (some students wondered about animals that can clone themselves). Teacher B recorded these three ideas on the poster and told the students that their homework was to observe animals in the neighborhood to see if they all looked alike.

While these examples show a snapshot of the science communities found in the classrooms of Teacher A and Teacher B, there are three important features of the communities to highlight as a foundation for this book and our work as science teachers. First, how Teacher A and Teacher B opened up or constrained opportunities for student talk set the tone for the remainder of the school year. Students pay attention to teachers' words and actions, and they notice how teachers respond to their ideas. Second, Teacher A and Teacher B sent different messages to students about what counts as a good statement to say out loud. By denying or valuing students' statements, teachers demonstrate to students what words and ideas matter, and what words and ideas should remain silent. Third, Teacher A and Teacher B treated the purpose of participation differently. Teacher A wanted students to say correct answers and complete predetermined practice problems, while Teacher B helped students to shape the direction of knowledge production in the classroom by asking for multiple hypotheses, generating and using language to describe a phenomenon, and by encouraging and supporting students to share ideas. Each of these features sends visible and invisible messages to students about what knowledge matters, how knowledge should be invoked and used in a classroom, and who is allowed to share ideas and claims to knowledge in a classroom.

TAKING STOCK OF SCIENCE COMMUNITIES IN CLASSROOMS

Teacher A and Teacher B are two examples from an ongoing conversation about science education. Building on research from the 1980s and 90s that called for students to "do" science in classrooms, reform efforts such as the Next Generation Science Standards have infused a slew of ideas about science teaching and learning into daily conversations among teachers, administrators, parents, and policy makers. Perhaps some of these ideas sound familiar: project-based learning, inquiry, hands-on, phenomenon, argumentation, explanation, modeling, and science practices. These ideas, along with many others, sound promising when encountered in professional development sessions, various journals, newspaper articles, and in conversation with colleagues. After all, people invested in science education, especially teachers and administrators tasked with designing science learning opportunities, care about students, their learning, and their science possibilities in the future.

Yet for all of this excitement about students "doing" science, resources for creating such sites of learning remain elusive. On a practical level, legitimate questions about concrete steps arise when attending professional development workshops, such as "How exactly do I create such classrooms and schools?" and "What are some actual tools and strategies I can use to plan and enact such learning opportunities?" On a conceptual level, deeper questions emerge, such as "What does it mean for students to do science?" "How do I help create equitable classrooms where students can do science?" and "What is the purpose of science classrooms and of learning science?"

CHANGING EXPECTATIONS FOR SCIENCE TEACHING AND LEARNING

If these questions sound familiar to you, you are not alone. Over the last two decades, expectations for science teaching and learning have rapidly changed, and often conversations about classrooms and schools shift at a faster pace than actual policies and actions in classrooms and schools. To provide a foundation for this book, let's focus on two important conversations that have big implications for any classroom and school community.

First, one pernicious image of teaching in need of disruption is the "sage on the stage," in which a very charismatic teacher delivers subject-matter information to students through various fact-laden presentations (or entertaining performances), which I refer to as "delivery pedagogy." The purpose of delivery pedagogy is information memorization and recitation: students are supposed to correctly recall and repeat facts stated by the teacher, textbook, or online source on various assessments. Beyond the obvious problem that delivery pedagogy is boring for students, this framing of science classrooms and schools also takes deficit views of students' thinking and experiences, framing their ideas as misconceptions and barriers to learning canonical content and practices. If students are positioned as inherently incorrect about their ideas and their experiences in the world, and the proposed solution is merely to tell students that they are wrong by presenting them with facts in the form of information delivery, then a classroom community has a deep trench from which to emerge.

Instead, a new vision of K–12 science education positions students as active producers of knowledge, as well as participants in scientific practices in classrooms, which necessitates shifts in science teaching. For example, teachers should design rich knowledge-building tasks that centralize students' existing and emerging thinking about the natural world as valuable resources for sensemaking.[1] Such a view of teaching is grounded in a research tradition about the role of students' community and culturally based intellectual resources in advancing knowledge building.[2]

A second crucial conversation in science education has been a focus on equity as a lens through which to see our work with students. While equity can take many forms, our friends and colleagues Jessica Thompson, Kirsten Mawyer, Heather Johnson, Déana Scipio, and April Luehmann offer a useful four-layered vision of equity for science teachers: (1) to recognize our own and others' worlds and developing critical consciousness; (2) to learn about and prioritize students' communities and community; (3) to design for each student's full participation in the community of science in ways that honor and leverage cultural and linguistic identities; and (4) to challenge the community of science through social and restorative justice.[3] By attending to equity in terms of providing opportunities for students to increasingly understand and challenge science as a discipline that has been powerfully useful and purposefully exclusive of marginalized people's ideas and experiences, teachers and administrators can help students see a more complete picture of how science can and should operate in the world. More importantly, students, especially from marginalized communities, can see that science, like any discipline, is made by people, is full of people's biases and assumptions, and should be constantly questioned and challenged to become a better way to understand the natural world.

These two conversations point to complex questions that we, as science teachers, must answer together: How can classrooms and schools support equitable communities that provide students with opportunities to do science, and to see that they can and should help transform the field? Most importantly, as a teacher or administrator, what is my role in supporting equitable science communities—what should I say and do to help students? These questions lie at the heart of this book. Regardless of buzzwords, policies that ebb and flow, and the latest popular assessment format, as a teacher or administrator, you play a crucial role in creating, sustaining, and growing classroom communities in which students feel safe and valued, and take on responsibility for science knowledge production and use over time.

DISRUPTING EPISTEMIC INJUSTICE

Regardless of the instructional frameworks, curricula, textbooks, and activities in use in schools, as teachers and administrators, you make decisions when planning, teaching in the moment, and during reflection that shape the classroom community in which students should shape science knowledge and practices. One lesson I learned while teaching is that as an adult positioned with authority in a classroom, I am granted immense power to provide explicit and implicit norms for participation and for naming what counts as science. Given this power and authority, we, as teachers and administrators, must make decisions about the messages we send to students about their participation and about science. Our words and actions, especially related to the treatment of students and their ideas, are foundational for creating equitable science communities in our classrooms and schools.

Given how important our words and actions are with regard to the treatment of students and their ideas, this book aims to help us see the creation and growth of science communities through a particular lens of inequity to disrupt: epistemic injustice. Briefly, epistemic injustice is a philosophical perspective, named by Dr. Miranda Fricker, that deals with inequities associated with knowledge and knowledge production practices.[4]

Ian James Kidd and colleagues provide example questions that arise when viewing institutions through a lens of epistemic injustice, which include: "Who has voice and who doesn't? Are voices interacting with equal agency and power? In whose terms are they communicating? Who is being understood and who isn't (and at what cost)? Who is being believed? And who is even being acknowledged and engaged with?"[5]

A primary concern with epistemic injustice in classrooms and schools is that students can be purposefully excluded from knowledge production and practices simply because of how people with power choose to see them and position them in the classroom. I argue that seeing science communities through the lens of disrupting epistemic injustice is crucial for four reasons:

1. Every person wants to be seen as a knower and contributor to knowledge production in some way. Students want to feel that they and their ideas matter to their peers and supportive adults. As illustrated in the example with Teacher A and Teacher B, how students and their ideas are positioned has immediate and long-term implications for individuals and the science community.

2. Too often, delivery pedagogy steers our work as educators toward deficit perspectives of students. As adults with authority and power, we must choose to see all students as amazing human beings with vast and wonderful life experiences that shape what they think and know, and as valuable contributors to the knowledge-making efforts of classrooms and schools.

3. In addition to seeing students as amazing and important people, we, as teachers and administrators, must establish explicit and implicit infrastructures to support students to feel safe and valued as important contributors to a science community. There are purposeful and public ways in which adults can demonstrate to students that they are the core of science teaching and learning in classrooms and schools.

4. Naming a specific problem around equity provides us with opportunities to see areas of success, to identify challenges, and to build a community of colleagues that can develop shared language and tools to grow together.

We will devote chapter 1 to exploring epistemic injustice and think extensively about how to disrupt epistemic injustice during moment-to-moment interactions with students, as well as on structural levels in classrooms and schools.

SUCCESSES AND CHALLENGES FROM REAL TEACHERS' CLASSROOMS

Too often, we are presented with imaginary scenarios, hypothetical situations, and thought experiments rather than actual concrete stories from classrooms and schools that might help us move forward with our work. To help illustrate the ideas in the book, and to show how real teachers have navigated the

9

complex work of creating and growing science communities, each chapter features examples of successes and challenges encountered by Anna Kramer and Lindsay Berk, two colleagues who have graciously agreed to share stories of their learning with and from students. I had the immense pleasure of working with Anna and Lindsay during their teacher preparation program, and I visited their classrooms quite frequently during their initial years of teaching. Many of the lessons I learned about disrupting epistemic injustice and creating science communities emerged by watching Anna and Lindsay deftly navigate teaching, form strong relationships with students, and continually learn with and from their students' communities and experiences.

Anna earned her master's in teaching from the University of Washington, where she learned a lot about justice, equity, and her position of privilege as a white woman in the teaching profession. Anna is in her twelfth year of teaching middle school (having taught grades 6, 7, and 8), and is a National Board certified teacher. Anna began her career in White Center, Washington, and currently lives in Santiago, Chile, where she teaches at the International School Nido de Aguilas. Anna believes that all kids are primed to use scientific thinking to make the world a better place, are naturally curious problem-solvers, and learn when they connect with the natural world.

Lindsay brings fourteen years of experience in STEM curriculum design and project-based learning from upper elementary to graduate school students. She has taught environmental sciences to undergraduates while backpacking three hundred miles in the California wilderness, led middle school students on multiweek service learning in the Makah Reservation, and designed cross-disciplinary adventures in a project-based STEM high school. For the last four years, Lindsay has found her niche in the middle school science classroom. She has led "Passion Projects" based on student interests, engaged students in Socratic Seminars, and coached Science Olympiad teams in robotics, aviation, and forensics. As a cofounder and science facilitator at the Millennium School, she incorporates her background in wildlife biology, geographic information system (GIS), and outdoor education into multidisciplinary projects with real-world application. Lindsay is a graduate of The University of California, Los Angeles, with master's degrees from the University of North Carolina–Chapel Hill and the University of Washington.

Given their scope of experiences and grade levels, Anna and Lindsay provide important insights about building on successes and navigating challenges for teachers and administrators across middle and high schools.

Each chapter will include a vignette of Anna and/or Lindsay related to the theme of the chapter, grounding the ideas in concrete examples from their actual classrooms. Importantly, the vignettes will feature episodes of classroom talk illustrating how teachers work to recognize, value, and move forward with student ideas to disrupt epistemic injustice. In addition, each vignette provides descriptions of instructional materials and artifacts designed by the teachers to facilitate the disruption of epistemic injustice in classrooms. While the focus of the book is not explicitly on instructional materials, illustrating how Anna and Lindsay used particular practices, talk moves, tools, and assessments will provide a stronger foundation for teachers and administrators to support their learning (as well as the learning of colleagues) to transform classrooms and schools.

THE WORK AHEAD

This book's aim is to empower us, as teachers and administrators, to reimagine the purpose of science teaching and learning, and to serve as a resource for people at middle and high school levels to initiate immediate and long-term changes to classrooms and schools. More importantly, this book can help teachers and administrators see classrooms and school through the perspective of disrupting epistemic injustice, which can change how science, teaching, and students are framed in science classrooms. In brief, this book is about helping teachers and administrators see and open up opportunities for student participation rather than shutting down students' ideas and experiences.

There are two main audiences for this book. The primary audience is those who have the most immediate opportunities for interactions with students—middle and high school classroom teachers. A main purpose of the book, then, is to provide teachers with a guide and resource they can read and immediately use to shift the community of classrooms in terms of teaching, learning, and science. In addition, the book can serve as a resource for teachers as they engage in study groups, district professional learning opportunities, and conversations with colleagues locally and nationally. A second audience for the book is people who help design learning opportunities for preservice and in-service teachers (such as instructional coaches and teacher educators), and those who create policies about teacher professional development and certification (such district-level policy makers, officials at state departments of education, and local or national legislators). This book can also serve as a resource to consider what, how, and why students and teachers should learn over time, and how they might collect evidence of student learning and teacher success.

The onus is on us, as teachers and administrators, to help colleagues and students learn to recognize and act on moments with the potential to disrupt, rather than perpetuate, epistemic injustice in science classrooms. This book will advance four radical and connected shifts in teaching and learning that will help us, as educators, better support each other to begin to disrupt epistemic injustice. First, this book will help educators shift colleagues' visions of teaching toward purposefully centering student thinking as the main driver of learning, and to thinking about the creation of science communities as an interactional accomplishment between people in classrooms and schools. Second, in order to shift their stance on teaching, this book provides concrete tools and practices for helping teachers and administrators notice students' ideas as crucial resources for the science work in classrooms. Third, this book provides teachers and administrators with ideas and resources for professional learning opportunities to rehearse the process of disrupting epistemic injustice by attending and responding to students' ideas. Fourth, through the process of noticing, attending, and responding to students' ideas, teachers and administrators can shift their instructional practice in ways that recognize and address the power and positionality that they can use to perpetuate or disrupt moments of epistemic injustice.

This book is divided into nine chapters. The first chapter describes epistemic injustice and names instances in which epistemic injustice might be observed in schools. The second chapter highlights the major conceptual challenges and solutions of disrupting epistemic injustice in classrooms; this sets the conceptual groundwork for the book. Chapters 3 through 6 provide educators with examples from actual classrooms where teachers I have observed and collaborated with are engaged in this work. In addition, each chapter includes concrete questions, exercises, actions for educators to consider and use in schools. Chapter 7 proposes recommendations for people outside class-rooms and schools, such as scientists and policy makers. Chapter 8 is a space in which Anna and Lindsay share their experiences and suggestions as you begin the work of reimagining classrooms and schools. Finally, chapter 9 suggests how to use this book in collaboration with colleagues, including conducting action research on your collective work and learning. I am thankful that you are thinking about important ideas around teaching and learning, and I look forward to the journey with you as we create equitable classrooms and schools while disrupting epistemic injustice.

ONE

Confronting Epistemic Injustice

AS WE BEGIN our journey in thinking about classroom communities, be sure to recognize your prominent role in the lives of children and their families. As an adult in a position of power in a school, you represent how and why science matters in students' lives, and you set the tone for how classroom communities develop and grow over time. The work you are doing, and how you are engaging with colleagues around building and growing science classroom communities, is monumentally important.

Given how crucial you are for building and growing science classroom communities, we should remember the three reasons why disrupting epistemic injustice is important:

1. Every person wants to be seen as a knower and contributor to knowledge production in some way. Students want to feel that they and their ideas matter to their peers and supportive adults.
2. Too often, delivery pedagogy steers our work as educators toward deficit perspectives of students. As adults with authority and power, we must choose to see all students as amazing human beings with vast and wonderful life experiences that shape what they think and know, and as valuable contributors to the knowledge-making efforts of classrooms and schools.

3. In addition to seeing students as amazing and important people, we, as teachers and administrators, must establish explicit and implicit infrastructures to support students feel safe and valued as important contributors to a science community. There are purposeful and public ways in which adults can demonstrate to students that they are the heart of science teaching and learning in classrooms and schools.

To start thinking about science classroom communities in which students feel valued, safe, and eager to engage in science, we must first consider how schools are situated in society. Given how society chooses to treat students, especially from communities that are purposefully marginalized by people with power, we will then think about how epistemic injustice is an outcome of such actions.

SCHOOLS AND SOCIETY: CREATING CONDITIONS FOR EPISTEMIC INJUSTICE

While this book focuses on epistemic injustice and the creation of classroom communities in schools, we must remember that schools are designed by people with power and often reflect the norms and values of dominant groups. Therefore, epistemic injustice is an outcome of larger inequities that skew how people in power learn to see the world. For example, epistemic injustice can result from sociopolitical and economic inequities that emphasize White, Western, heteronormative, individual, and masculine values that shape how we all—intentionally or unintentionally—might develop biases toward people who are part of different communities and cultures.[1]

Situating schools in larger society helps us think about the importance of seeing and valuing students who enter classrooms. While we often hope that schools might be places that welcome all students, we know that all students do not enter science classrooms with equal positions in relation to each other because of entrenched social and political power structures.[2] In particular, marginalized students are often treated as though their knowledge and ways of acting are less important or irrelevant, and are often positioned as the opposite of how people should act and know in schools.[3] Marginalized students also experience the compounding historical experiences of microaggressions, as well as the policing of behavior and thinking. Even if marginalized students are superficially invited to participate in sensemaking activities, teachers and administrators might still regulate their thinking and actions, thus shutting down their attempts at participation.[4] Therefore, classroom communities in which students' ideas have value, and in which each person supports each other's learning and participation, can be difficult to create, examine, and describe, yet we know they are essential for students.

EPISTEMIC INJUSTICE

Given the importance of creating science communities in classrooms and knowing that schools are sites that create opportunities for inequities to occur, let's turn our attention to a specific form of inequity that can arise in classrooms, and which is crucial to disrupt: epistemic injustice. Before we think about this construct and what such ideas mean for building classroom communities, there are three important points to establish.

First, the work of understanding relationships among knowledge, communities, and interactions between people is not new. Colleagues have long examined how and why some people's knowledge matters in certain settings while others' knowledge is dismissed (including Lilia Bartolomé, Gloria Ladson-Billings, Paulo Freire, Henry Giroux, Na'ilah Nasir, and Danny Martin). We should continue to learn from and build on their extensive research. Second, while this book is focused on knowledge-building practices in relation to science communities, people's identities are inextricably intertwined with conversations about equity and participation. How dominant groups choose to position others as capable (or not) of knowledge production is shaped by perceptions of identity. Third, pondering complex ideas is always better when colleagues think together. I encourage you to form discussion groups, to design and try out learning opportunities, and to think collectively about instruction in order to learn with and from each other.

Defining Epistemic Injustice

Let's first define epistemic injustice, and then we will think about how such a lens can help us see inequities in classroom communities. The term epistemic injustice was coined by philosopher Miranda Fricker. Broadly, epistemic injustice involves inequitable treatment that relates to issues of knowledge practices, communication, information, and truth.[5] Ian James Kidd and colleagues provide example questions that arise when viewing sites through a lens of epistemic injustice: "Who has voice and who doesn't? Are voices interacting with equal agency and power? In whose terms are they communicating? Who is being understood and who isn't (and at what cost)? Who is being believed? And who is even being acknowledged and engaged with?"[6]

Thus, epistemic injustice illuminates issues of credibility, authority, and testimony with regard to how people are treated as knowers by people with power and by each other.

Forms of Epistemic Injustice

Epistemic injustice is enacted in at least four forms. Let's look at descriptions of the forms and consider examples that could occur in science classrooms.

1. Testimonial injustice. Perhaps the most visible form of epistemic injustice, testimonial injustice occurs when someone trying to speak has their idea dismissed by a person with power. From the perspective of a person with power, testimonial injustice occurs when someone silences or suppresses speech of marginalized people. Over time, testimonial injustice can lead people to feel that they are not allowed to participate in knowledge practices.

As an example, think back to the interaction described in the introduction between Teacher A and the student who never spoke in class. As the adult and the person with authority in the classroom, Teacher A clearly has power. When the silent student finally spoke, Teacher A could have stated that the student had an important idea or could have asked the student to expand on their thinking. Instead, Teacher A chose to dismiss the student's idea. As noted, this student never spoke in class again, likely because they felt their ideas were useless and irrelevant. By positioning the student's idea as "unscientific," Teacher A sent a message to students about which ideas mattered and which ideas were incorrect. Other students took note of this interaction, as Teacher A performed a form of coercion by compelling students to speak and act in ways that aligned with preferred forms of participation in the class.

2. Hermeneutical injustice. Perhaps the least familiar, hermeneutical injustice occurs when people are unable to make sense of their own experiences, or to explain their knowledge to others in society. Often, such injustice occurs because people with power purposefully restrict access to ideas they think are problematic. If society never hears ideas from marginalized people, then such people may not know how to express their needs since they are never heard.

Hermeneutical injustice could involve public statements or actions against marginalized people, yet such people cannot make sense of the inequity, given how a community chooses to limit what is possible to be known. For example, imagine a classroom with a White teacher who has a diverse class with many Black and Brown students. The teacher wants students to see images of famous scientists and feel inspired, so the teacher puts up posters of White men and women as exemplars of science knowledge. During conversations about science phenomena, students attempt to share ideas and knowledge from their communities. However, the teacher dismisses such ideas as "misconceptions" and "not scientific." In this classroom, the teacher is sending explicit and implicit messages to students about what counts as science knowledge and about what scientists look like through images of success. Students in this class might feel uncomfortable since they do not see Black and Brown scientists and are told that their ideas are incorrect, but they may be unable to explain why they feel wronged. If the teacher's words and actions are never questioned, and if success in the class depends on a recognition of the teacher's version of science, then the community may perpetuate hermeneutical injustice since students are not provided a context in which to understand how inequities are enacted against them.

3. Intrapersonal injustice. This form of epistemic injustice occurs when people with power do not allow their views to be informed by people they choose to marginalize.[7] In these cases, people with power do not understand how to listen to the ideas from marginalized people, nor do they choose to learn from people who might challenge dominant norms.

Intrapersonal injustice often results from biases that people with power develop about who is smart, whose ideas matter, and who will be successful in a classroom. For example, if a teacher believes certain students are disruptive, that their ideas are wrong, and that they cause interruptions to class time, this teacher will likely not be primed to hear the student's ideas as important for the class community.

4. Hierarchical injustice. Sometimes, people with power can inflict hierarchical injustice when they create infrastructures to ignore, distort, and discredit knowledge practices that run counter to dominant norms.[8] Within infrastructures, features such as artifacts and standards represent the knowledge and practices that people with power choose to value.[9]

In science classrooms, we can imagine that hierarchical injustice could be perpetuated by using representations, such as posters and "word walls," that indicate correct ways of speaking scientifically. Worse, we can imagine that if a student speaks in a way that the teacher does not consider scientific, the teacher might reference the posters and word wall as a guide for correct talk. Thus, the teacher bans students' ways of talking and upholds the ban by surrounding students with the ideas and words the teacher deems correct without any input from the students.

Taken together, these four forms of epistemic injustice allow people with power to purposefully exclude certain individuals and communities from knowledge production while simultaneously creating and mandating participation in the very institutions that enforce an inequitable epistemic hierarchy.[10] Over time, such participation can lead to marginalized people becoming trapped in cycles of epistemic oppression in which they are seen as unreliable speakers and as incapable of knowledge production.[11]

FEELING EMPOWERED TO CHANGE CLASSROOM COMMUNITIES

As the mini-examples show, epistemic injustice can occur during moment-to-moment interactions between teachers and students, within a school as illustrated by the explicit and implicit norms for participation, and by promoting textbooks and standards that prompt schools to shut down students' sensemaking and knowledge practices. I hope none of us intentionally aim to harm students through repeated acts of epistemic injustice. We might think that we are doing students a favor by telling them when they are wrong about science so that they can learn correct ways of knowing and acting if they want to become scientists. However, as we have seen, such instruction often has the opposite effect, especially for students from marginalized communities. The more often students hear that their ideas and experiences are wrong, the more likely they are to internalize that what they think and know is unimportant to their teachers and classroom communities. This creates a rift in thinking for students—the knowledge that is valued in school is not the knowledge that lives in local cultures and communities. In particular, when White ways of knowing are elevated above Black and Brown ways of knowing, this reinforces a terrible history of epistemic oppression.

What can we as teachers and administrators do to help disrupt epistemic injustice and create wonderful, vibrant, equitable science communities in schools? At first, the question might seem daunting. After all, how can one teacher or one administrator dismantle a century's worth of schooling aimed at promoting particular knowledge and practices by suppressing knowledge that might seem dangerous to people in power? Rather than become overwhelmed by changing systems of schooling, a better place to start is to wonder, "Given my position of power in my school and district, what I can do, with colleagues, to start making changes where I am right now?" As teachers and administrators, you are positioned with power to serve as educational leaders and innovators in your school and district. Students will enter your classrooms tomorrow, next week, and next year. As educators, we know that our words and actions make a huge difference in the lives of students. Therefore, this book will help us all think together about changing classroom communities by disrupting epistemic injustice. Hopefully, we will feel empowered to take immediate actions and to consider future possibilities, as we work together to reimagine our classroom communities.

DISRUPTING EPISTEMIC INJUSTICE: AN EXAMPLE FROM LINDSAY'S CLASSROOM

One powerful reason to name actions and the denial of knowledge-based opportunities as epistemic injustice is so that we can start to use a shared language to describe problems, and so that we can collectively reimagine and redesign classroom communities as places that recognize and value children as burgeoning knowers and to gain their trust as people who care about their well-being and ideas.[12] Let's look at what we as educators should think about by looking inward and outward, and then we will dive into an example of disrupting epistemic injustice in Lindsay's classroom.

Looking inward, as educators, we must recognize that intentionally or unintentionally, we might dismiss students' ideas because our biases make us unable to value the words and knowledge that lie outside our understanding of the world. We must recognize that as people with power, our words and actions have huge implications for the classroom community. We should actively unearth biases in whose knowledge matters and how such knowledge is recognized as valuable, and should never dismiss words, experiences, and practices of students as unimportant. In addition, we must prime ourselves to hear and learn from students about our biases, because students, especially from marginalized groups, can articulate assumptions and prejudices that people with power may not recognize.[13]

Looking outward, there are at least four disruptions to epistemic injustice that can help transform classroom communities:

- Name specific groups of people who are harmed and how they are harmed. Such naming is especially important to confront generic language of helping all children learn. For example, designing interventions to help all children does not unearth how daily inequities built into society (such as racism, sexism, and classism) result in disproportionate acts of epistemic injustice inflicted on marginalized children, especially those from marginalized communities.
- Create and examine opportunities for beneficial epistemic friction, in which students and adults from various knowledge systems interact, work together, learn to understand and value each other, and create shared meaning together.
- Learn to engage in virtuous listening, which includes knowing when to remain silent, when to suspend judgment about knowledge and knowledge practices, calling critical attention to one's limited experiences and interpretative expectations, and letting marginalized students create the dynamics for classroom interactions.
- Actively design and leverage anti-oppressive epistemic resources to undermine and change oppressive institutional structures.

By considering inward and outward steps toward disrupting how epistemic injustice transpires, we can begin to examine and dismantle the structures and institutions that people with power purposefully built to advance dominant forms of participation.

Lindsay and the English Ivy Unit

Now that we have considered some examples of epistemic injustice, let's peek into Lindsay's classroom to see how she purposefully and actively worked to disrupt epistemic injustice during an ecology unit that occurred during the last six weeks of school. Lindsay's example helps us see what classrooms can become if adults and students work together and actively employ disruptive actions to reimagine science classroom communities.

Before diving into the unit, there are three important features to note. First, the unit occurred at the end of the school year. Recall that in the introduction, I discussed the importance of the beginning of the school year as helping to establish, sustain, and grow science-learning communities. Over time, the work of valuing students' ideas and experiences and providing opportunities for them to shape the practices, talk, and participatory structures of the community opens avenues for disruption of epistemic injustice on bigger scales. Second, the progression of the unit—from initial planning to the co-construction of science with students—unfolded in ways that Lindsay could not have predicted when first planning the unit trajectory. Third, Lindsay learned with and from her students as they ventured out into the local community, blurring the boundaries of where science takes place and elevating questions about whose ideas have significance when working on a puzzling community-based problem.

To frame the ecology unit around something specific her students could explain over time, Lindsay selected invasive species as an anchoring phenomenon. Lindsay had two primary goals for the students. First, she wanted her students to describe how and why invasive species altered ecosystems. Second, Lindsay wanted students to consider the preventive steps scientists and community members could take to halt the of spread invasive species once they became established in a particular ecosystem. While pondering her unit plans, Lindsay decided to take daily walks through the students' communities, looking for examples of invasive species she could incorporate into the unit. During her walks, Lindsay discovered English ivy (*Hedera helix*) enveloping buildings, trees, and other plants.

To learn more about English ivy in the area, Lindsay called local scientists who worked for the city government and asked if they had data on why English ivy seemed to successfully outcompete native plants. However, the local scientists told Lindsay that they did not collect any data; instead, they just tried to kill the ivy when possible. Disappointed, Lindsay decided to tell her students about the unit plan and the lack of government data so students could help inform her next pedagogical decisions.

During the first conversation about English ivy, Lindsay described her observations of the English ivy in the surrounding communities and relayed her conversation with the local government scientists, highlighting their decision to not examine the invasive plant in their community. After several students asked questions about why the local scientists might ignore the ivy, one student raised his hand and asked, "Can we study the ivy and show the government what we find out?" Surprised, Lindsay agreed and subsequently decided to recast her unit to let students take on the role of lead investigators.

Days one and two. The unit began with groups of students constructing initial explanatory models to theorize about the English ivy's success as an invasive species in their community. Each group drew various features of an ecosystem, as well as the English ivy, and wrote accompanying hypotheses and lingering questions about the plant's success. At this point in the school year, the students knew that they would revise the initial models based on evidence they gathered over the course of the unit.

The next day, Lindsay and her students ventured out into their community to collect samples of both English ivy and native plants that the ivy covered or grew near. While in their community, some students suggested that they photograph the various locations of all the English ivy plants they could find in order to make "some kind of map." Lindsay agreed and provided the students with a GPS device so that they could record latitude and longitude for the plants that they photographed. Using the photographs and latitude and longitude records, Lindsay worked with several students after school to create a GIS map of the English ivy in order to produce a different representation of the data they collected. One immediate feature of the map that became clear was that the ivy was found throughout the students' neighborhoods, which housed many marginalized families. However, the ivy was not found in parts of the city where wealthy families lived. Students began to wonder why this difference occurred.

Day three. In addition to conducting a community walk and taking photographs with latitude and longitude locations, students marked places where they wanted to return in order to collect plant samples of both native plants and the English ivy. The purpose of the sampling would be to gather evidence on why the ivy outcompeted native plants. Before collecting the samples and designing the experiments, Lindsay and her students co-constructed a list of seven hypotheses about the ivy's success that they could test in their classroom. Each hypothesis had to meet three criteria that the students and Lindsay codeveloped during a classroom discussion:

- *Plausibility.* Each hypothesis had to have a high likelihood of occurring (i.e., ivy was brought into the region as a decorative plant and successfully started to spread), rather than seeming highly unlikely (e.g., aliens planted the ivy to destroy Earth).
- *Aligning with data* Each hypothesis had to incorporate data and ideas from ecology, rather than dismiss important concepts (e.g., ivy is outcompeting plants because it is a predator and physically eats them).
- *Testable.* Each hypothesis could be experimentally tested in a classroom setting, rather than proposed without consideration of how to gather data (e.g., ivy is outcompeting the native plants because the ivy's atomic bonds are stronger, therefore making the ivy stronger).

Student groups volunteered to collect samples, design experiments, and test each of the seven separate hypotheses: ivy crowds other plants; ivy "strangles" or takes air; ivy takes water; ivy blocks sun; ivy takes "nutrients"; ivy releases chemicals; ivy blocks pollinators.

Days four, five and six. After collecting samples of native plants and English ivy, students engaged in a two-part experimental design process. First, each group planned an experiment to test one of the seven hypotheses. In this experimental design, they stated their evidence base for the hypothesis, the process by which they would test a specific hypothesis, and the potential data they could collect based on the results. Second, students conducted a peer review of other groups' proposed experimental designs, ensuring that the data from the experiment would both provide evidence for the explanatory model and not be the result of errors in the experimental design. After peer review, the student groups revised their original experimental plan.

Following the experimental design process, Lindsay helped the students run the experiments to test the seven hypotheses. In one experiment, they planted several different specimens using different soil, light, and water conditions, and monitored the results. When the experiments concluded, the student groups compiled the data and attempted to make claims based on the evidence they generated. After the initial sensemaking rounds of experimental data, student groups conducted another peer review of the claims, triangulating the experimental data, the claims, and the hypotheses. Throughout this process, Lindsay facilitated multiple small group conversations and helped elevate certain ideas to the public plane of talk in the classroom.

Days seven and eight After the gathering of experimental data, Lindsay provided an opportunity for the classroom community to revisit the seven original hypotheses. This process had two components. First, Lindsay appropriated a tool from a colleague, called a "red light/green light tool," to help students strengthen their seven hypotheses. The red light/green light tool is a poster placed on the classroom wall that students use to judge the strength of hypotheses using evidence from activities. "Red light" refers to the act of using evidence to refute a hypothesis, whereas "green light" is when a hypothesis is bolstered with evidence. Using the red light/green light tool, students evaluated the hypotheses based on the evidence they collected during the experiments.

The second component of revisiting the seven hypotheses was that students noticed that no single hypothesis accounted for English ivy's success as an invasive species. Subsequently, students began to synthesize hypotheses, noting the difficulty of explaining English ivy's success using a limited range of ideas and evidence.

Days nine and ten. After the synthesis of hypotheses, Lindsay's students revised their initial models to incorporate the new evidence and ideas they compiled throughout the unit to explain the English ivy's success in outcompeting the native plants. As with the initial models, students drew components of the model, wrote long, complex explanations of the phenomenon, and noted lingering questions that they wanted to continue to investigate. In particular, students wanted to know more about the disparity between the ivy's success in their communities and the seeming absence of ivy in wealthier areas. Lindsay was pleased by students' insistence that the final explanation of the English ivy phenomenon was complicated, noting, "I'm glad they see that ecology is complex, and they couldn't have seen this without doing the science themselves" (observation debrief).

After revising their explanatory models, Lindsay and her students reconnected with an admittedly stunned local government official who was impressed by the students' engagement with science beyond recalling facts. Lindsay hoped that as students took on the role of scientist in her classroom, they would see the "boundary of the science classroom and their community blurring a bit—I think students can do science that impacts their community in my class" (observation debrief).

Seeing Lindsay's Classroom Community Through Epistemic Injustice

Lindsay and her students codeveloped a powerful and equitable science community in their classroom that enabled them to think about invasive species through a lens of local needs and interests. Let's look at the English Ivy unit through the lens of epistemic injustice to consider how Lindsay and her students disrupted images of what is possible in science classroom communities.

- *Name* specific groups of people who are harmed and how they are harmed. Lindsay and her students explicitly noted that English ivy, which was an invasive species that the local government did not prioritize as a problem, seemed to be overtaking the native plants in students' communities, not in wealthier areas. Rather than dismissing students' concerns, the question of why ivy was successful in some parts of the city became a class-wide wonderment throughout the unit.
- Create and examine opportunities for beneficial *epistemic friction*. Lindsay and her students created such opportunities during class by analyzing each other's experimental designs—creating and revising models—and by

deciding on science practices such as hypothesizing. Importantly, Lindsay and her students also created opportunities for epistemic friction by contacting and reconnecting with local scientists about the students' work. Such conversations helped steel the students' desire to engage in the research and helped shift the scientists' understanding of the science work and the students as people who should shape science practices.

- Learn to engage in *virtuous listening*. Lindsay could have dismissed students' requests to engage in the ivy research, could have dictated how the experiments and practices would unfold, and could have steered students toward the explanation that she wanted to hear. Instead, Lindsay listened to students' needs and requests, and opened up opportunities for them to share ideas and shape the science practices.
- Actively design and leverage anti-oppressive *epistemic resources* to undermine and change oppressive institutional structures. Lindsay and her students created resources to represent knowledge (maps and models), and knowledge practices (hypotheses criteria, red light/green light) that allowed them to push back on narratives about teaching and learning science, and about local ecology. Additionally, Lindsay and her students shared the resources with local scientists to shape how the scientists viewed ivy and their future work.

By purposefully working to disrupt potential episodes of epistemic injustice, Lindsay and her students reimagined and codeveloped a different classroom from many typical spaces in schools. In the classroom, Lindsay and her students codesigned opportunities to:

- *Challenge classroom science focused on information acquisition.* Lindsay encouraged students' science ideas, including their models, hypotheses, experimental proposals, and challenges to the teacher's knowledge, rather than expecting them to simply absorb facts, procedures, and other correct answers.
- *Take and use authority.* Lindsay provided students with opportunities to assume expert roles by defining, proposing solutions, and resolving problems that emerge during complex science work. In addition, all members of the classroom community had authority to shape science activity, rather

than Lindsay positioning certain students as better or more knowledgeable than others.

- *Students hold each other and the teacher accountable.* Lindsay and her students codeveloped a classroom community in which students held each other and the teacher accountable to others and to the emerging science-learning norms. By "holding accountable," I mean that students took up the agency to question Lindsay's pedagogical decisions, to hold reflective conversations about the nature and direction of the science practices, and to negotiate solutions to conflicts that emerged during the course of the science work.
- *Build trust.* Working toward the ivy unit allowed students to trust that Lindsay actually cared about them, their ideas, and their lived experiences. Students also began to trust that Lindsay actually wanted them to engage in science that they codeveloped rather than being mysteriously steered toward a correct answer that the teacher secretly withheld throughout the unit. As educators, we must recognize the importance of building trust to disrupt epistemic injustice and reimagine classroom communities.

These opportunities did not occur randomly or accidentally. Lindsay designed initial learning opportunities for students, placed value on their ideas, and worked with students to shape the classroom community over time. If students experience science as a predetermined set of procedures and facts, they could come to believe that they can only participate in science as technicians, those who conduct the routine work of experiments, and are not permitted to participate in knowledge practices. As philosopher Helen Longino noted: "While the official picture of a field presented in its textbooks is the picture of a uniform and consistent understanding, the background from which this understanding emerges contains alternative interpretations of the data included in the textbook picture as well as data inconsistent with it. The selection represents ... what a society (those in society with the power to effect their preferences and privilege their needs) thinks it should know or wants to know."[14] In other words, society and schools, thus far, want to bound students' participation in science by limiting their vision of what their role can and should be in the discipline.

Lindsay, however, worked toward a different kind of science community in her classroom in which all students shape the work that is done. Lindsay thought that students could help disrupt epistemic injustice. This is a particular value—the power of positioning all students as important members who should shape science practices in a community. Rather than science, and society, becoming a hierarchy in which technicians (i.e., students) and others are put in lower and less powerful positions, science can teach students that their ideas can and should have a bearing on how and what knowledge develops within science communities and how that knowledge is communicated to and received by society.

TENSIONS AND DILEMMAS

Before moving on, we need to recognize that disrupting epistemic injustice and creating powerful science-learning communities is complex work. When you and your colleagues start to think about how to reimagine teaching, learning, and the classroom communities that sustain students' cultures and practices, tensions and dilemmas will inevitably arise. Let's name three of the tensions and dilemmas so that we can consider them as we work toward reimagining science classroom communities.

How Should Ideas Shape a Science Community?

As you begin thinking about reimagining science communities, remember that you and your collaborators might think differently about how and why students' ideas should shape the science that occurs in the classroom. As people with power in schools, you may not instantly agree about how to design science communities and how to disrupt epistemic injustice. Moving forward, important questions arise, such as: How should ideas from marginalized knowers shape our classroom and school? What criteria can we use (or develop) to ensure that multiple ideas and ways of knowing are honored and used in our school? Can our school support novel science communities, or are changes needed so that students feel valued and represented in the building?

Does this mean "equal time"? One of the debates that you have likely encountered is around the equal time of controversial ideas—that students should encounter ideas that may promote harmful and dangerous notions in order to provide multiple perspectives. However, sometimes people who promote equal time are actually part of dominant groups and can perpetuate epistemic injustice under auspices of marginalization.[15] For example, some dominant Christian groups want creationism to be taught alongside biology, for prayer to be part of daily classroom routines, and for Bible study to be offered in American public schools. However, such requests have been denied in multiple court cases.[16] While dominant Christian groups might claim marginalization in schools, their lawsuits and actions perpetuate epistemic injustice. By showcasing dominant Christian versions of history in public sites as canonical knowledge and by dismissing non-Christian epistemologies as invalid, such groups perpetuate colonialist actions that have occurred for millennia.[17] From a bigger picture, such calls for equal time attempt to purposefully harm others, to assert norms that limit participation, and to espouse false narratives about the world. Therefore, as teachers and administrators, we must ask what is marginalized, in what ways, and in relation to whom? How do we ensure that the voices of the most impacted are elevated rather than those who claim oppression in order to perpetuate injustice?

Are there correct answers? Finally, a common worry that teachers and administrators might express is that they want students to know the correct answers about science phenomena so that they can make informed decisions about their life. This concern is reasonable, especially in an era of misinformation around devastating global disasters such as the climate crisis and the COVID pandemic. However, there are two important ideas to consider. First, science knowledge is constantly changing. What we consider "canonical" was not seen as correct decades ago, nor will correct answers today be the correct answers of tomorrow. As humans constantly learn more about the natural world, our understanding of nature and of each other changes. Therefore, I ask that you and colleagues consider these questions: What is science knowledge for? Why are students positioned as correct or incorrect about their understanding of the world? What does it mean to be wrong in our understanding of the natural world? Second, disrupting epistemic injustice is less about correct and incorrect answers, and more about providing students, especially from marginalized groups, with opportunities to shape the knowledge and practices of a classroom community. Allowing multiple voices to participate in asking questions, designing investigations, analyzing data, and reporting results creates a more expansive and better version of science than if participation is limited to dominant groups of people. Therefore, we should ask: What does it mean for students to really shape science in the classroom? How can we create opportunities for science to become more expansive rather than limited?

CHAPTER EXERCISES: LOOKING BACKWARD AND FORWARD

As you and your colleagues think about how you might disrupt epistemic injustice to reimagine the classroom communities in your school, considering how past and present injustices may harm students is important when planning for the future.

Questions to consider with colleagues

1. When have I supported students' ideas by opening up possibilities for participation? How were these examples different from when opportunities for students were shut down?

2. What words, ideas, or actions do I want to promote in a classroom? How do those words, ideas, or actions align with, or differ from, what students say and do in classrooms? How do I feel about the similarities and differences?

3. When a student shares an idea that seems unusual to me, what is my first thought and reaction? How can I prepare myself to hear students' ideas as important?

4. Why might students feel unsafe to share ideas in my classroom or school? What may have happened in the past that shapes the present?

5. How might I design a classroom community to open up opportunities for students' ideas to shape the thinking and actions of other students (and me, as a person with power)?

6. Do we treat all students' ideas with the same importance? If not, which students are we more likely to ignore and dismiss? Why?

7. Which students may be marginalized in our school? How do we know? Why might they be marginalized?

8. What are some explicit words I can say, and actions I can take, to show students that I care about them and their ideas?

9. What resources and tools do we need to support students' participation, especially students from marginalized groups?

10. How might we have dismissed students' communities and experiences in the past? How might we have honored students' communities and experiences in the past? How can we show students that we are listening to and valuing their communities and experiences?

TWO

Pernicious Myths About Science and Teaching Classrooms That Limit Opportunities for Students

NOW THAT WE'VE DONE some initial thinking about building science classroom communities and disrupting epistemic injustice, let's turn our attention to how schools might create conditions for inequities to persist. In this chapter, we will explore three myths about science and schools that, when left unquestioned, perpetuate the conditions for epistemic injustice to exist. Such myths restrict opportunities for students to share and discuss ideas, to shape science practices, and to learn with and from each other (as well as teachers and administrators) as they name and examine problems to solve. Instead, we will think about how to show students a different vision of science teaching and learning, using examples from Anna's and Lindsay's classrooms. As with every chapter, thinking and talking with colleagues about the ideas and exercises is highly recommended.

MYTH 1: SCIENCE

Here's a quick exercise: Close your eyes and, without pausing to think, imagine a successful scientist. Next, try talking out loud to a colleague or write down what you see in your mind. Who is this scientist? Where are they? What is around them? What assumptions do you make about their race, economic class, gender, and sexuality? When I completed this exercise before writing the words, my answers were: an older, heterosexual, upper-middle-class White man in a laboratory surrounded by expensive equipment (and no other people to help him out). Clearly, my instant image of science needs reimagining, but also reflects the messages about science that I have been inundated with over the years. Maybe like you, I thought I was a successful participant in science because I achieved good grades and can readily recite information memorized from science courses. However, few of us have ever truly experienced the daily practices of science fields, nor have we examined why science fields conduct and report research in the ways that seem correct to us. Therefore, we need to confront three assumptions about what counts as science, and we need to ask hard questions about why some people are allowed to participate in science, while others are excluded from full participation.

Assumption 1: *Science is separate from society.* During the era of COVID and the climate crisis, people often claim that science is (or should be) separate from larger society. Science, people argue, is an objective field that should not be tampered with by outsiders, should not be used for political gain, and should not be shaped by the agendas of powerful people. While optimistic at best, the perspective that science and society are separate ignores the long history and reality of how science serves, and is shaped by, people, politics, and cultures. Look no further than debates about climate change, and how branches of the federal government were banned from even using the term during the Trump administration.[1] Further back in US history, industry lobbyists shaped conversations about regulating known dangers to people, such as cigarettes and asbestos, by hiring teams of scientists to create research that upheld the lobbyists' goals of deregulation (for further conversation, please see the book *Merchants of Doubt*).[2] Therefore, we need to think about science as part of social, political, and historical contexts in order to understand how scientific disciplines operate, and how certain people play a key role in deciding whose ideas matter—or do not matter—in the creation of science knowledge.

Assumption 2: *Science is open to everyone.* Schools are places where we tell students that anyone can be a scientist when they grow up. While I hope such a story will match reality in the coming years, historically, very few Black and Brown students, as well as women, were allowed to enter science fields.[3] There is an important distinction to make here: while science—a means of investigating the natural world—is open to everyone via many lenses to investigate phenomena, the opportunity to work as a professional scientist (or have research regarded as professional) is often closed off to many people.

Often, such exclusion is by design and is perpetuated by two main barriers. First, in many countries, science is the domain of older White men, and they publicly and purposefully work to exclude many people from participation in the disciplines. Even if people other than White men carve out space to work, White men readily erase them from narratives about scientific discoveries. Second, as feminist philosophers note, White men often shape the conceptual, epistemic, material, and social practices of science, excluding voices of other people.[4] As an example of both barriers, Rosalind Franklin was a crucial contributor to efforts to understand and photograph the structure of DNA. However, her confidential research was shared without her permission with the two White men given credit for DNA's structure (Watson and Crick), and she was not awarded a Nobel Prize despite her efforts and her work fueling the research of scholars who won the prize (Watson, Crick, and Franklin's adviser, Maurice Wilkins).[5] Thus, as a profession, science can perpetuate epistemic injustice by purposefully leaving out many people from larger conversations about science practices and processes.

Assumption 3: *All science is the same.* We often speak about science as a universal field in which everyone agrees on the knowledge, practices, and norms for participation. Schools often fuel this assumption, advertising a singular scientific method ("the scientific method"), promoting simple and linear investigations, and claiming that all science has a nature that is inherent to the field. However, as philosophers, historians, and sociologists note, every field of science and their subdisciplines have different knowledge goals, practices, and possibilities to communicate the ideas. Even the cultures of science spaces differ from place to place, and how science is conducted in one laboratory may be very different from how science is conducted in another laboratory.[6] Thus, conversations across science fields can be difficult, and agreement about key ideas may not be evident. For example, ask a physicist, a chemist, a biologist, and an earth scientist to define and describe the idea of "energy." Likely, you'll receive four different answers, even though each person is a scientist. Or, think about whether a microbiologist and an astrophysicist can conduct the exact same science. While a microbiologist can create a control group of bacteria to put away for later examination, an astrophysicist does not have a similar option when examining planets and galaxies. These examples show the importance of understanding how different forms of science operate, and demonstrate how communication about science may fall apart, even among professional scientists.

Given these assumptions, we need to recognize that there are many ways to think about, and many avenues for examination of, the natural world. We must also recognize how epistemic injustice can thrive when these assumptions about science limit how we see the world and how other people choose to examine nature. Certainly, in science, there are constant conversations about what counts as good practices. We need to remember, however, that those conversations occur between people who have biases, agendas, ways of seeing and knowing, and histories that are shaped by different contexts. As the philosopher Donna Haraway likes to say, there is no "god trick" in which scientists can remove themselves from the natural world they are trying to observe and explain.[7] Science is, and always has been, made by people, shaped by politics and society, and purposefully exclusive of certain ideas (most recently, since the Renaissance, science excludes ideas that challenge Western, White, heteronormative, and masculine norms for participation).[8] Creating powerful science classroom communities, then, means that we have to provide avenues and opportunities for students' ideas to shape the science work, rather than shut down the ideas as unscientific, a move associated with efforts to maintain epistemic injustice.

Examples from Lindsay

Let's look into Lindsay's classroom to see some examples of how she, as a teacher positioned with power, actively uses talk moves and actions to question myths and assumptions about science in order to disrupt epistemic injustice in the classroom.

Lindsay often uses two overlapping actions to open up science avenues for students rather than constrain the image of science that students encounter. During investigations of puzzling phenomena, Lindsay asks students to use large poster paper to create representations of their thinking. These tools, called face-to-face tools, are visual anchors for the students' constantly evolving ideas. Here is a list and description of the tools Lindsay uses. Anna uses these tools as well. You can visit also visit the "Ambitious Science Teaching" website (see endnote for link) to learn more and to see pictures of the tools in classrooms.[9]

- *Red light/green light.* A poster placed on the classroom wall that students use to judge the strength of hypotheses with evidence from activities. "Red light" refers to the act of using evidence to refute a hypothesis, whereas "green light" is when a hypothesis is bolstered with evidence (recall the tool from Lindsay's ivy unit example).
- *Whole class model.* A poster on the classroom wall where an initial explanatory model is drawn and written, and that changes over time as teachers and students revise the model.
- *Small group models.* The same as the whole class model except students work on these during small group conversations.
- *Sticky notes.* Small pieces of paper that can adhere to other paper. Students use sticky notes to revise part of an idea, add a new idea, remove an idea, and ask questions about part of the model.
- *Summary table.* A chart placed on the classroom wall that lists the activities the students engage in during a unit and provide space for linking evidence from the activity to an explanation for some puzzling phenomenon under investigation.

Lindsay's use of the tools helped show students that the ideas can and should shape the science practices and direction of the classroom.

Lindsay's second action is to use public and purposeful talk moves to help students feel safe to share ideas, and to work together as a community. Often, Lindsay invokes the classroom as a safe place when making public statements about the constant generation and revising of hypotheses. For example, a common discursive exchange between Lindsay and her students often involved disrupting the notion of right or wrong answers:

STUDENT: I know we set up the experiment to test our idea [that ivy blocks out sunlight from other plants], but what if it's wrong?

LINDSAY: What do you mean by "wrong"?

STUDENT: What if blocking sunlight is not important? Then we just wasted everyone's time.

LINDSAY Look around you at your ideas on the wall (*Lindsay points to the representations of student thinking*). This is how messy science works. Sometimes hypotheses help explain a phenomenon. Sometimes hypotheses help revise our ideas by telling us what is not a part of the explanation. If your experiment shows that blocking sun is not a reason for the ivy's success, then we can still revise our posters based on your important finding.

Note how Lindsay eases the student's worry—that they might get the wrong answer—and instead makes the sharing and recording of ideas the norm for participation.

In another example, Lindsay tells students that she wants them to "participate as scientists in a knowledge-making community because that's how scientists make sense of their back-and-forth work of testing and revising ideas." Such community work required that she design her classroom to allow collaboration between students. Lindsay, therefore, purposefully places students in groups rather than have them sit individually. She also allows students to move between groups when discussing ideas, creating space for students to easily walk back and forth between tables. For example, if different groups converge on similar ideas, Lindsay asks the groups to meet and discuss their findings. In addition, during designated times, students can freely move back and forth between tables, comparing models and hypotheses with other groups. Thus, Lindsay classroom's provides students with opportunities to engage in messy science work across sites.

Disrupting Epistemic Injustice in Lindsay's Classroom

Over time, the actions Lindsay (and Anna) took to help students see science and their participation differently helps to disrupt potential epistemic injustice by redefining "who knows" in a classroom science community and to make science a very public endeavor instead of private work. As a public endeavor, teachers and students codevelop science practices over time. To negotiate a public science community, Lindsay and Anna, along with their students, position each other as responsible for everyone's learning and for the science work.

This negotiation begins at the start of the school year when Lindsay and Anna create a safe space to share ideas rather than make the classroom a place where ideas are shut down.

MYTH 2: TEACHING

Similar to science, teaching invokes a certain image and means of interaction between an adult and their students. If you imagine teaching, what do you see? White men acting as rule-bending sages in *Dead Poets Society* and *School of Rock*? White women attempting to save urban youth, who are often portrayed as troubled Black and Brown students, as in *Dangerous Minds* or the *Freedom Writers*? Every one of us, given our many years of participation in some form of schooling, have developed an internal story of what we think teachers do and think about. Our superficial observations of real teachers become entwined with a mythologized version of teachers in popular films, such as those mentioned.

However, our superficial observations and the movies extolling (often White) fictional teachers as a savior of marginalized students in underserved schools obscure the professional preparation and work of real teachers, especially with regard to the daily work of creating and sustaining equitable learning communities in classrooms. For example, one pernicious image of teaching in need of disruption is the "sage on the stage," in which a very charismatic teacher delivers subject-matter information to students through various fact-laden presentations (or entertaining performances), which I refer to as "delivery pedagogy." The outcome of delivery pedagogy is often that students are supposed to correctly recall and repeat the curriculum's facts on various assessments. This version of teaching is ripe for epistemic injustice, as the teacher and the curriculum are the sole authority of talk, action, and knowledge.

To begin the process of disrupting epistemic injustice through the creation of equitable learning communities, we must build a new image of instruction. Rather than view teaching as a set of pedagogical actions to control what students think and regulate their participation in disciplinary work, we need to reimagine teaching as a profession in which teachers value students, their thinking, and their participation. Such communities upholding students' ideas as resources for sensemaking creates the potential for more equitable and inclusive learning, especially for children from marginalized communities. In these communities, teachers account for inherent power structures of classrooms, which position the teacher as content and pedagogical authority. Teachers purposefully signal to students that their ideas have value, and teachers' talk and actions shape students' perceptions of themselves and their peers about who can and should participate in science knowledge production. Finally, teachers open up opportunities for students to shape science knowledge and practices rather than shut down the ways in which students want to frame and explore the world.

An Example from Anna

As we revisit Anna's classroom, we should consider an important question: How are our talk and actions as teachers directly related to the opportunities we provide students to shape science knowledge and practices? Let's look at an example from Anna's classroom to see how our colleague challenges the myth about teaching as delivery pedagogy to create powerful science communities. Anna wanted to show students that creating science knowledge can be a process of tinkering rather than reciting correct answers. She understood that, as the teacher, she needed to provide opportunities for students to engage in different forms of talk and action than in classrooms where they individually worked on reproducing answers valued by the curriculum.

For example, in a unit about energy transformations, Anna arranged the tables so that students could collaboratively build, test, revise, and critique models of potential and kinetic energy in roller coasters. Anna separated the tables, keeping the spaces in between them open. The purpose of the openness was to "allow students to move between groups and talk to each other—if they can't move around, they can't share ideas." Sometimes, Anna heard students talking on opposite sides of the classroom and knew they would benefit from a conversation with each other. I often observed her say, "[Student 1], please walk across the room and talk to [Student 2]. You should both hear each other's ideas because you need pieces of what the other is saying." Note two features of Anna's comment. First, Anna's classroom allowed students to transport ideas across space and time rather than isolate ideas at separate tables. Second, Anna's classroom did not bound students' participation to one specific location; students worked together, across space, to tinker with the science of the classroom.

Disrupting Epistemic Injustice in Anna's Classroom

Whenever I participated in Anna's classroom, I was struck by how aware she became of her power and desire to change the norms of schooling for students. As the teacher, Anna took purposeful and public actions, often telling students why she wanted them to take charge of the science community rather than defer to her as the sole authority. Anna told me that a key to this teaching was that she became increasingly comfortable with uncertainty about what students might say and do, as well as her upcoming actions as a teacher. However, this public navigation of uncertainty helped students see that Anna really did care about their ideas, and truly wanted their help in shaping the science and teaching in the classroom.

MYTH 3: EQUAL OPPORTUNITIES FOR ALL STUDENTS

The third myth is that schools and classrooms provide equal opportunities for all students to become successful science learners and participants. On the surface, and when facing the public, schools often try to portray themselves as great equalizers of opportunities for children. The message is that no matter who students are and where they come from, school is a place that rewards hard work, and that anyone can propel forward in society by achieving academic success.

While ideal in sentiment, such meritocratic notions mask entrenched inequities that hinder opportunities for marginalized students to achieve the same levels of participation as their White peers. We are learning that perhaps the most crucial assumptions to disrupt are entrenched notions about whose knowledge and forms of participation are valued in classrooms. A common adage many new teachers adopt is that "all students can learn science concepts." While noble in rhetoric, not all students are seen as equally smart, capable, or motivated because of historic and purposeful sociopolitical power structures. In particular, marginalized students are consistently treated as though their knowledge and ways of acting are less, or irrelevant, and in fact are not aligned with school norms and dominant paradigms of science.[10] By privileging some forms of knowledge and participation (likely those that align with a teacher's view of the world) under the guise of equal opportunity for all, epistemic injustice is perpetuated.

An important principle of teaching to consider moving forward is that we must build strong relationships with our students to work toward understanding their lives and experiences. An important avenue for building relationships with students is to forge strong ties between teachers' experiences in schools and students' communities outside school. Hopefully, as teachers and administrators, we are invested in similar goals as students' community members: better opportunities for students. As teacher and administrators, we need to spend meaningful time in our students' schools and communities—not as saviors or the sole experts, but as learners about the histories, values, cultures, and experiences of students. Such actions also help communities see that their knowledge and experiences make an impact on schools and the future of their children.

An Example from Anna's Class

As we revisit Anna's class, let's notice that her talk and actions to build relationships with students, as part of a larger plan to create powerful science communities, are not random or miraculous. When the school hired Anna, she immediately looked at the demographic information and asked the school secretaries to tell her about the students. Anna learned that her school comprised many families who had migrated to the United States (within one to two generations), in particular, families from Mexico and several countries in South America, and from multiple Pacific Islands. Anna asked community members to help her learn about students' lives and histories, and spent time at community events during the summer before school began. She also engaged in dialogues with herself, trying to unearth her biases and assumptions about the students' lives. Anna's work to confront her biases and to learn more about the students' communities allowed her to prime herself to listen for, and value, ideas that students invoked from their communities.

To begin the school year, Anna taught about the seasons, a required curriculum topic. Rather than use her department's activity (watching a video), Anna decided to leverage some of her Pacific Island students' lived experiences as resources for the class. She asked students to describe qualitative observations about summer and winter in both Samoa and in the Northwest region of the United States (the location of the school). Note that Anna, in her first unit, tried to establish a classroom norm of having students' science ideas and experiences play a prominent role in the classroom community.

During an initial class, Anna used students' ideas to make an instructional decision in the moment, changing the lesson based on student thinking. Anna and her students began class by reviewing data from a computer simulation, which provided information about the amount of sunlight and temperature at different places on Earth during the year. During this discussion, Anna decided that, based on student ideas (some students thought that Earth was "sometimes tilted," while other students thought that Earth was "always tilted"), the class needed to revisit the computer simulation to discuss their competing theories. By revisiting the computer simulation, Anna gained more opportunities to hear students' thinking about their science ideas.

Anna also worked to establish her classroom as a safe space for students to share science ideas from their own lived experiences because she wanted "see their thinking so I know where to go"—in other words, use students' science ideas as a resource for shaping her practice. One talk move Anna utilized to help students feel safe sharing ideas was to note that their ideas were valuable resources for their learning. In this example, Anna and a student discussed the seasons based on the student's lived experiences:

ANNA: Where does the temperature change as earth is tilted?

STUDENT: I don't know.

ANNA: What about the equator? At the equator . . .

STUDENT: The temperature doesn't change much.

ANNA: When you did the computer simulation and selected for a whole year's temperatures, what did you see?

STUDENT: Not much change in temperature.

ANNA: What about looking at [the Northwest] for a year?

STUDENT: Yeah, the temperature changed a lot.

ANNA: What's the difference?

STUDENT: If the earth stayed at zero degrees if it wasn't tilted, the temperature wouldn't change in [the Northwest].

ANNA: OK, so I hear you saying that if the earth wasn't tilted, [the Northwest] wouldn't experience temperature change. Is that related to your life? Do changes in [the Northwest] temperature according to the computer data make sense with what you know in real life?

STUDENT: Yes, because if the earth wasn't tilted, I'd only need to buy the same kinds of clothes—the temperature wouldn't change.

ANNA: So you're starting to explain to me why the earth is tilted using both your experiences and data. That's powerful for you and for science.

In addition to giving Anna access to student thinking, this interaction provided students with evidence that Anna valued their ideas and lived experiences, and wanted to hear their thinking. Thus, Anna both enacted her plan from the beginning of the school year to create a safe classroom community and provided opportunities for students' ideas and experiences to shape the instruction and direction of the community.

Lessons from Anna's Example

Anna's purposeful work to examine her own biases to learn more about students' histories and communities, and her actions to help students' lives and experiences become valuable resources in the classroom are hallmarks of efforts to disrupt epistemic injustice. By looking internally at her initial ideas about students, and providing external efforts through talk moves, tools, and instructional practices to help students feel safe and valued, Anna helps us see that opportunities for marginalized students to become strong innovators of science in classrooms takes the purposeful efforts of teachers and administrators. The forging of strong relationships does not happen by accident, and by seeing the classroom as a community to build and grow, we begin to see the initial and ongoing actions we must take to confront who we think is smart, who we think should contribute, and how a science community should grow over time given the emerging ideas and needs of students.

BIG THEMES

The three myths, along with the examples of how Lindsay and Anna actively and openly questioned the myths with students, provide a useful foundation for conversations about science communities. As we saw in the English Ivy example from chapter 1, as well as examples in this chapter, disrupting epistemic injustice and creating classroom communities in which assumptions about science, teaching, and equitable learning opportunities are questioned and reimagined requires concrete actions from teachers and administrators. Lindsay and Anna took purposeful steps to continually develop a classroom community with students as equal partners in determining the culture and practices. All this became possible because Anna and Lindsay developed an equity lens to see their professional work as providing rigorous and equitable learning opportunities for students that are also culturally sustaining, while enacting core teaching practices (using tools) to take immediate actions in classrooms. This combination of reimagining science, teaching, and equitable learning opportunities allows teachers to:

1. Attend to culture, and equity of opportunity for all students.
2. Anchor students' ongoing learning experiences in complex and puzzling science phenomena.
3. Use students' everyday ideas, experiences, and questions as resources within the classroom community to advance everyone's thinking.
4. Legitimize students' participation in, and codevelopment of, ensembles of science practices to test ideas they believe are important to their developing explanations and models of the world.
5. Provide daily opportunities for students to reason through productive talk.
6. Give students access to specialized tools and routines, and codevelop tools and routines with students, that support their attempts at science-specific forms of writing, talk, and participation in activity.
7. Make students' thinking public and subject to consideration by the classroom community.
8. Sequence learning experiences to help students integrate ideas together and revise understandings of big ideas of science fields.

These interconnected elements provide a broad picture of teaching in powerful classroom communities that reimagines the purpose and roles of powerful adults in schools (again, see the "Ambitious Science Teaching" website for more details and for a discussion of these principles).

THINKING TOGETHER

One important message to take away from our collective work is that the creation and growth of strong learning communities can begin in your classroom and school today. While implementing one talk move or one tool could be a good start, the ways in which we treat students as human beings, how we value their ideas, and how we feature their preferred forms of communication and actions can begin the process of reimagining and changing the opportunities and places for students to learn. No matter your role in a school, you have the responsibility to help shift communities and provide students with different and better equitable opportunities.

Anna's and Lindsay's classrooms show us that, as people with power, we represent the type of science, teaching, and version of equity that we value in schools. To both reflect the myths and assumptions about school we pondered in this chapter and to take actions to reimagine our communities, let's walk around the communities we shape: classrooms, schools, or other sites of learning. On our walk, let's notice what is visible or invisible about our values around science, teaching, and equity. How do we choose to represent what counts as science, teaching, and equity to students? How might these representations perpetuate epistemic injustice? While you can do this work alone, as always, I recommend taking this walk with colleagues to share ideas out loud and to think together about what you notice. Here are some suggestions for activities to engage in and questions to ask during the walk.

Sketch or print a map of the school building. As you walk, mark places on the map where:

- Science currently occurs
- Teaching currently occurs
- Efforts at equity currently occur

Some questions to consider:

1. How are science, teaching, and equity represented to students in terms of messages and physical space (posters, displays, public student work, and beyond)?

2. What explicit and implicit messages about science does the school promote? Who makes decisions about the type of science messages that are displayed?

3. What explicit and implicit messages about teaching does the school promote? Who makes decisions about the type of science teaching messages that are displayed?

4. What explicit and implicit messages about equity does the school promote? Who makes decisions about the type of equity messages that are displayed?

5. Where and how (if at all) do messages about science, teaching, and equity overlap?

6. Given your school map, what might students think about how science, teaching, and equity are related? On a schoolwide level, what are some initial actions to take to shift the explicit and implicit messages about science, teaching, and equity that students observe and hear?

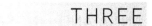

THREE

Looking in the Mirror

Auditing Assumptions About Science Classrooms and Students

WHEN THINKING ABOUT designing classroom communities that support students and that disrupt epistemic injustice, a great first question we might ask is: Where do I begin? This book, and our work together, cannot offer easy solutions. I realize that other books, professional development sessions, and videos often prescribe step-by-step solutions and linear fixes to problems in schools. However, as we are noticing, creating powerful classroom communities requires a different stance about teaching and learning than we might have previously imagined. This is not easy work, but creating and growing powerful classroom communities is an important opportunity that we must take seriously.

There are two processes required to reimagine classrooms: looking inward at our vision of teaching and our lenses through which we see students, schools, and science, and looking outward to consider how our words and actions open up or constrain possibilities for students. This chapter focuses on looking inward, which works in concert with other chapters about looking outward. The primary focus of this chapter is to provide examples of how we might learn from students to help us grow as teachers, and to help us ask questions about what we value in science classrooms. Thus, this chapter will help us audit our assumptions about what we think could and should be happening in our science classrooms.

ANNA AND LINDSAY EXAMPLES

Anna and Lindsay provide help for us all because they demonstrate how, even when attempting to enact ambitious and equitable instructional practices, there is still so much to learn from students about teaching. Both examples described here occurred at the beginning of the school year as Anna and Lindsay began building relationships and communities with students. Like all transformative events that disrupt epistemic injustice, Anna's and Lindsay's words and actions helped show students that their ideas, experiences, and communities would be treated as valuable and crucial for the classroom community.

Anna and Mayan Lunar Information

Like many middle school science teachers, Anna's curriculum mandated that students learn about the moon's relationship with earth. Since her school was close to the ocean, Anna planned a unit around tides, which she hoped would help students feel more connected to their local beaches. On the first day of the unit, Anna asked students to consider the relationship between the moon and tides. While some students noted that they had a passing memory of the moon having something to do with tides, two young women (after whispering together in the back of the room) raised their hands. They decided to tell their peers about their Mayan ancestry, informed the class that Mayans had a deep understanding of the moon and tides, and would ask their families for information to bring to the class the following day.

Anna did not plan for, or anticipate, that two students in her class had Mayan ancestry and would care deeply about connecting their families' history to the class discussion of the moon and tides. However, in that moment, Anna realized three actions she needed to take as a teacher: (1) acknowledge and thank the two students for their contributions, (2) express genuine excitement to learn from the students' families and cultural knowledge, and (3) learn more about the Mayan culture and its relationship to the moon since she needed to better understand the students' ideas.

Over the next two weeks, the Mayan students brought in new information each day about the moon, which Anna and the class positioned as vitally important to their understanding of local tides. For example, when looking at tidal data about high and low tides, Anna and the Mayan students asked the class to consider how their families' information might align with, and inform, the locally produced tide charts. Anna also asked the class to include information from the students on the final assessment to link cultural practices to curricular science. In the meantime, Anna conducted her own research about Mayans and the moon and, by the end of the unit, made a purposeful decision to publicly thank the two students for teaching her about the science from their communities.

Lindsay and Cancer

Lindsay also encountered a seemingly mundane topic in the curriculum—cell division—and considered how to make cell division relevant to students' lives. Lindsay noted that cell division is often presented as a series of steps, but the importance of the steps is often described without context. Therefore, Lindsay decided to have the students think about cell division in the context of cancer, considering what happens when cell division is not halted by typical mechanisms. On the first day of the unit, Lindsay told students that they were going to learn about cell division, and then she asked students about cancer. Lindsay anticipated hearing students' ideas about cancer from a clinical perspective—what cancer is, how cancer spreads, and possible cancer treatments. Lindsay did not expect students to make the conversation deeply personal, sharing stories of friends and family who survived or died from various forms of cancer.

Like Anna, Lindsay felt her mind was whirring as students began to share stories of aunts, mothers, fathers, cousins, and best friends who had cancer. Rather than shut down students' stories as irrelevant, Lindsay recognized this moment as a point of departure that she needed to honor. Lindsay listened intently as student after student shared stories of cancer, and how some forms of cancer seemed more treatable than others. By the end of the conversation, Lindsay told students that she was reimagining the purpose of the unit. Rather than focus on cancer strictly from a cell division perspective, the class would think about the biology, epidemiology, and sociology of cancer: What is cancer, how can we stop cancer, and what are the human and cultural impacts of cancer? Lindsay and the students decided that their homework was to ask their family members about loved ones who had cancer. What type of cancer did they have? What treatments had they received? How did doctors talk to the families about cancer? Did the families feel supported by the medical industry while receiving cancer treatment?

Over the next few weeks, Lindsay and her students learned about cell division and cancer, and also noticed that the medical industry never fully explained cancer to their families. Lindsay and her students recruited local cancer survivors to share their journey with the class, and to think about what the community wanted to know about cancer. Many families knew about terms such as "tumor" and "malignant," but no one helped families make connections between cell growth, division, and cancer. Students felt empowered to take medical knowledge back to their communities and became adamant that they would be able to help future community members who received a cancer diagnosis. At the end of the unit, Lindsay publicly thanked the class for teaching her about cancer, their families, and their communities.

Lessons from Anna and Lindsay About Looking Inward

Anna's and Lindsay's similar experiences offer four lessons for us to consider as we think about disrupting epistemic injustice in our classrooms and schools:

1. Anna and Lindsay recognized that students' words and stories represented points of departure from instruction and schools that value content coverage and answers that directly align with a curriculum. Rather than shutting students down, Anna and Lindsay listened, adapted their teaching, and thanked students for teaching them. By recognizing and acting on points of departure, Anna and Lindsay opened up opportunities for students' ideas, lives, and communities to shape the classroom.

2. As White women in positions of power as teachers, Anna and Lindsay realized that they needed to be better primed to listen to and learn from students and their experiences. Therefore, they chose to spend time in students' communities, learn from community members, and build strong relationships with students in order to begin redistributing their power and to disrupt epistemic injustice. Thus, Lindsay and Anna did not view themselves as the central authority of science and pedagogy. They wanted to redistribute power to students.

3. Anna and Lindsay publicly linked their instructional adaptations and learning to students' stories and experiences. They thanked students for

teaching them and noted how students' ideas helped shape the classroom community.

4. Anna and Lindsay both realized that how they presented science seemed separate from people's lives and experiences. Instead, students helped them realize that science is not a cold and clinical bubble outside people's lives. Science is inseparable from society and communities. These experiences set the foundation for future units, such as Lindsay's ivy unit.

Each of these lessons helps us look inward and ask important and hard questions about what we value around science teaching and learning in classrooms.

AUDITING OUR ASSUMPTIONS ABOUT SCIENCE TEACHING AND LEARNING

After looking into Anna's and Lindsay's classrooms, a next important step to creating powerful classroom communities is to begin auditing our assumptions about science teaching and learning. By auditing assumptions, I mean that as colleagues, we must ask questions about our definitions of good teaching and learning, about science, and about students' roles in shaping the pedagogical and disciplinary work in classrooms. For example, an assumption about learning we might hold is: "I give the grade of an A to students who try hard in my class." On the surface, this assumption may seem fair. We must give grades, and as teachers, we often have some capacity to make decisions about which students receive certain grades. Taking a stance that students who try hard should receive an A may also seem reasonable because we might be accounting for circumstances beyond our control with regard to student participation. As teachers, we may hope and expect students to do their best, and if they do not try hard, we can place the blame on their shoulders and reduce their grade.

However, let's practice our audit of assumptions by asking several questions about working hard equating to receiving an A. First, what do we mean by "work hard"? What are our criteria for defining hard work? For example, does working hard mean that a student has completed all required assignments? Does working hard mean that students spend a certain amount of time studying, or participate in certain ways in our class? Second, what counts as an A?

Does an A signify something about students' mastery of disciplinary knowledge and practices? Could a student who demonstrates science understanding (according to our assumptions about science understanding), but does not work hard, still receive an A in our class? Could or should a student who works hard but does not demonstrate content understanding receive an A?

Stepping back for a moment, we can see that stating one assumption about hard work and grades unearths a host of questions about our definitions and stances around teaching and learning. This is the work we must continue as we disrupt epistemic injustice and reimagine classroom communities. For this chapter and book, I recommend using two guiding principles from my friends and colleagues Jessica Thompson, Kirsten Mawyer, Heather Johnson, Déana Scipio, and April Luehmann that I briefly mentioned in the introduction as a starting point to audit our assumptions about teaching, learning, and science.[1]

First, as teachers, we need to recognize our own and others' worlds and develop a critical consciousness. As teachers and administrators, we must recognize and accept that we are positioned with power in schools. This recognition carries multiple simultaneous meanings. Our power and position in schools means we take on the awesome responsibility for helping children feel safe and valued, and helping them learn. Parents and communities entrust their children to us, and we should assume the professional responsibility with a sense of pride and hope. This realization is at the core of creating powerful classroom communities.

We must also realize that our power and position might create biases and skew how we learn to see the world and treat children, their ideas, and their community resources. In particular, if we are White teachers and administrators, we must think deeply about who we are in relation to our students. If you are like me, you may have learned about science (and perhaps teaching) as separate from conversations about race, class, cultures, and communities. As noted in chapter 2, science has a long history of being positioned outside peoples' biases and society's power structures. Therefore, from the perspective of epistemic injustice, we need to interrogate our ideas about who can or should do science and whose ideas are scientific. Some potential questions we might ask ourselves include: How can I learn more about my students' experiences? How can I be responsive to my students' context? How can I audit my own assumptions and examine how my privilege and power are a part of this situation?

Second, we must learn about and prioritize students' communities and cultures, especially as we consider the concepts and phenomena to use in classrooms. For example, there has been an important push to make science more relevant to students' lives. However, teachers might attempt to impose relevance onto the phenomena that a class examines. Rather than assume we know the topics and phenomena that students should learn, as teachers and administrators with power, we must work with students to brainstorm questions, problems, and phenomena they want to investigate.

Sometimes, negotiating science means that phenomena and questions are grounded in students' lived experiences and community needs. Recall Lindsay's ivy unit in which the questions, science practices, and communication were all situated in students' immediate community. In this example, situating the science in a local issue prioritized places, people, and languages that were familiar to students. Other times, teachers and students may decide that they want to learn about phenomena and ask questions from a different and faraway location. For example, Anna and her students took a great interest in learning about hurricanes as they followed the weather of the southeastern United States even though they all lived in the Pacific Northwest region of the country. In this example, Anna and her students wanted to step outside their local communities to learn more about people and places that were facing immediate hardships.

Regardless of the locality of science, the creation of classroom communities in which students' voices shaped the science to be learned helped disrupt epistemic injustice as students saw that their ideas, voices, and values were needed to advance the community's work. Our most important task as teachers and administrators is to build and grow communities with students in which the plurality of students' cultural identities and community experiences provides the foundation for the science that happens in communities. As adults with power, we have the responsibility to build relationships with each student, to learn about the communities in which their school exists, and to ensure that every student has opportunities to infuse their cultures and experiences into the classroom.

CONCLUDING ACTIVITIES

Next, we will engage in four tasks that help us audit our assumptions about science, teaching, and students. We will also consider how to take concrete steps toward disrupting epistemic injustice by reimagining and recreating our classroom and school communities. As with every task, our learning is enhanced as we think, talk, and learn with colleagues.

Task 1: Science Assumption Audit

First, write an initial definition of "science." A sentence frame could be: I define science as ____.

Next, try to explain the initial definition of science. Where did the definition come from? A sentence frame could be: This is my initial definition of science because ____.

Now, let's work on diving into our definition of science by auditing some assumptions that may be visible or invisible in our definition (see table 3.1).

TABLE 3.1 **Visible and invisible assumptions about science**

Question to ask	Our initial answer to the question	Observations and lingering questions we have about this visible or invisible assumption
What counts as science? Who decides?		
How is science knowledge made?		
Who can do science? What supports or barriers exist for people to do science?		
What is "good" science? What is "bad" science?		
How should science change over time?		
How should science be communicated to other people?		

After answering the questions in the table, let's revise our initial definition of "science." A sentence frame could be: I now define science as ____.

Finally, let's publicize our thinking about our revised definition of science. How did our definition change, and why? A sentence frame could be: I revised my initial definition of science because ____.

Task 2: Teaching Assumption Audit

Next, let's write an initial definition of "teaching." A sentence frame could be: I define teaching as ____.

Next, try to explain the initial definition of science. Where did the definition come from? A sentence frame could be: This is my initial definition of teaching because ____.

Now, let's work on diving into our definition of teaching by auditing some assumptions that may be visible or invisible in our definition (see table 3.2).

TABLE 3.2 **Visible and invisible assumptions about teaching**

Question to ask	Our initial answer to the question	Observations and lingering questions we have about this visible or invisible assumption
What counts as "good" teaching? Who decides?		
What is my role in the classroom? Why?		
How do I have power in the classroom and school?		
What evidence of teaching do I provide to others about successes and challenges in the classroom?		
What are my most important class norms? Why?		
What role do students play in shaping my instruction? Why?		

After answering the questions in table 3.2, let's revise our initial definition of "teaching." A sentence frame could be: I now define teaching as ____.

Finally, let's publicize our thinking about our revised definition of teaching. How did our definition change, and why? A sentence frame could be: I revised my initial definition of teaching because ____.

Task 3: Student Learning Assumption Audit

Finally, let's write an initial definition of "student learning." A sentence frame could be: I define student learning as ____.

Next, try and explain the initial definition of student learning. Where did the definition come from? A sentence frame could be: This is my initial definition of student learning because ____.

- What counts as learning in my classroom? Why? What evidence of learning do I collect and value as a teacher? How can my definition of learning shift over time?
- What kind of student do I call on and why?

Now, let's work on diving into our definition of student learning by auditing some assumptions that may be visible or invisible in our definition (see table 3.3).

TABLE 3.3 **Visible and invisible assumptions about student learning**

Question to ask	Our initial answer to the question	Observations and lingering questions we have about this visible or invisible assumption
What counts as student learning? Who decides?		
How do I know a student is smart? Why?		
What knowledge and practices are important for students to learn? Why?		
Who do I want students to become in my classroom? What identities should they begin to develop?		

Question to ask	Our initial answer to the question	Observations and lingering questions we have about this visible or invisible assumption
Which students usually participate in class, and which students usually do not participate? Why do I think that there is a difference?		
How do I want student participation to differ from the beginning of the school year to the end of the school year?		

After answering the questions in table 3.3, let's revise our initial definition of "student learning." A sentence frame could be: I now define student learning as ____.

Finally, let's publicize our thinking about our revised definition of student learning. How did our definition change, and why? A sentence frame could be: I revised my initial definition of student learning because ____.

Task 4: Build Asset Perspectives of Teaching, Learning, Students, and Communities

Now that we have done some thinking and writing about our assumptions, we can consider how to move forward and take first steps to disrupt epistemic injustice and see students' ideas, experiences, and cultures as foundational for classrooms. There are two collective tasks we can try: writing an autobiography of your science learning in school, and cocreating an asset map with students and people from the community.

Given their powerful principles for examining our assumptions, Jessica Thompson and colleagues also push us to think about how our experiences as students in schools and science classrooms likely influence our definition and actions in science teaching and learning.[2] They suggest two ideas for helping us remake classroom communities. First, they urge us to write about how our emerging understanding of power and privilege was shaped by, and potentially enhanced by, the framing of science teaching and learning given our school experiences. I encourage you think about how your schooling shaped your current assumptions about science teaching and learning, and I hope as you begin the biography task, you consider big questions that emerge from our assumption audits, such as:

- Which people get to participate in what ways in my school and classroom? Why?
- How are hierarchies of power and agency established, explicit, and hidden? How might those change?
- What is my role in the classroom as a teacher? How can I shift my pedagogical framing and actions to build and grow science learning communities?

Second, Thompson and colleagues suggest that we create an asset map of local communities. Rather than drawing a map with deficits, perhaps noting the features of a community that we believe are missing, creating an asset map helps us see that what is valued in a community offers a lens into and connections with local culture. An asset map could include important community buildings (such as clubs, stores, churches, and organizations), as well as sites of historical significance as indicated by community elders. Taken together, auditing our assumptions, writing autobiographies, and creating asset maps (ideally created with students) help disrupt epistemic injustice by centering students' communities and experiences as crucial for the school's success while forcing us to reimagine what counts as science teaching and learning.

FOUR

Purposeful Talk Moves to Signal the Value of Students' Ideas, Experiences, and Communities

IN CHAPTER 3, we looked inward to audit our assumptions about science, teaching, and learning. We also began to reimagine how our planning, teaching, reflection, and classroom or school spaces can become better settings for powerful learning communities. In this chapter, we look outward by focusing on specific talk moves we can use, starting now, to disrupt epistemic injustice and open up avenues for participation. In chapter 5, we will examine a bigger picture of science practices and classroom communities.

Here we will examine daily, moment-to-moment interactions and talk moves that we can use with students to show them that we value their ideas, experiences, and communities. Learning from Lindsay and Anna, we will think about how to signal that we need students' ideas in our class rather than treating such thinking as "off topic" or "misconceptions." Such signaling—which should be explicit and public—is especially important during moments of uncertainty, when we might not anticipate students' words or actions. Such moments of uncertainty are key to building and growing classrooms communities. We can learn to recognize such moments and make principled pedagogical decisions so that students feel valued and heard by the teacher or administrator and their peers.

NAVIGATING UNCERTAINTY

Before we think together about specific talk moves during moment-to-moment interactions as well as science practices in the next chapter, I want to acknowledge that providing students with opportunities to shape classroom talk and actions, and to act on points of departure from instruction that perpetuates epistemic injustice, might initially feel unwieldy. Bounding the course of action and outcome before a lesson is comforting and safe. However, we need to recognize that society's images of teaching, and perhaps our teacher preparation programs, encourage control over students' thoughts and actions. As teachers, we often think (and are told) that we must design lessons to provide a visible pathway for student thinking while leaving a trail of clues for them to follow to arrive at our predetermined answer. Opening up opportunities for students to say and do things we cannot anticipate will hopefully help us confront and "de-settle" our assumptions about good teaching. As we have seen with our experiences in schools and in Lindsay's and Anna's classrooms, our talk moves as teachers and administrators are consequential for opening up participatory opportunities for students. Given that powerful classroom communities hinge on public discourse and building relationships with students, we must be prepared to notice and value student talk and actions as crucial for our collective learning.

Navigating uncertainty while still making sound pedagogical decisions is at the heart of professional teaching. As our friends and colleagues Eve Manz and Enrique Suárez note, while school presents an image of science as a linear and logical progression of experimentally proven facts, science in other settings must contend with a constant host of unpredictable factors.[1] Scientists, and teachers or administrators, must continually adapt talk and actions based on emerging factors. Our teaching, then, presents key opportunities to encounter unanticipated talk and actions, to make purposeful pedagogical decisions based on the emergent student discourse, and to move forward with instruction based on the decisions made in the moment. By navigating the uncertainty of teaching with students, and by using their voices to shape instruction, we can create a collective community of learning rather than frame science and success as individual enterprises.[2]

PURPOSEFUL TALK MOVES

Now that we have acknowledged the uncertainty of talk and actions as we disrupt epistemic injustice, we can think together about how our words (in this chapter) and bigger instructional actions (in the next chapter) start building strong classroom communities. Since we, as teachers and administrators, are positioned with instructional authority, we are often the mediator of talk and arbitrator of participation. Students, parents, and community members look to our signals about the kind of talk and actions that are valued in schools (in turn, I propose that we need to learn from students, parents, and community members about the talk and actions they want to see in classrooms; we should learn with and from each other). Therefore, as people with power in schools, we can disrupt epistemic injustice by clearly assigning value to students' ideas and experiences. By centering, elevating, and discussing student ideas, we make the norms for participation in our school public and clear: we value student thinking, experiences, and cultures.

Recall that many of the classroom stories we have examined so far are examples of points of departure in which Anna, Lindsay, or others encounter a participatory crossroads. Their words and actions might encourage or discourage student participation. In the examples in which our colleagues attempted to disrupt epistemic injustice, the teachers make public discursive moves to treat science ideas as resources for the community's science work rather than position them as right or wrong. Lindsay and Anna, for example, promote productive puzzlement, sensemaking talk, and reasoning, while simultaneously signaling that such contributions are welcome on the public plane of interaction. In counter-examples (recall Teacher A and the Punnett Square), teachers use talk moves to assign a value of correctness to student ideas, which prevents discussion by the classroom community. These teachers made clear to students that science ideas could only be treated as right or wrong answers and questions (i.e., students could ask wrong questions) that they either accepted or dismissed as irrelevant to their classroom community.

By using talk moves and actions to promote conversation or correctness, the teachers send signals to students about who is allowed to engage in creating and shaping science knowledge. For example, Lindsay and Anna purposefully and publicly tell students about the value of their thinking, and how their ideas add needed information and experiences to the classroom's collective understanding of the natural world. Thus, they are seeding the idea with students that they can and should shape what counts as science knowledge. Teacher A and others, however, steer students toward canonical facts found in textbooks and shut down avenues for participation that stems from students' lived experiences. In doing so, such teachers narrow what counts as science and send messages to students that science is only conducted in a certain way that has historically and purposefully excluded many people. Thus, our words and actions about student thinking make a huge difference in helping students see possible participatory paths as people who can shape science knowledge and practices, or as people who must mimic ways of knowing and doing that are privileged by people with power.

To make these ideas concrete, let's return to Lindsay's classroom for an example of how her talk moves can open up opportunities for student participation rather than constrain their thoughts and perpetuate epistemic injustice. As always, context is needed for the example. At the beginning of a school year, Lindsay's class was focused on why some mutations result in genetic disorders. Lindsay, knowing the importance of her words and actions, made purposeful and public statements about students' ideas and experiences. For example, if Lindsay ever needed to inject content in a conversation, she routinely began such talk by saying, "I won't be up here [talking] for long … You will practice working with your own ideas."

When talking with students in small groups, Lindsay helped students make sense of content and consider next steps in the following brief exchange.

LINDSAY, *to Student 1*: See, [Student 2] is using evidence.
STUDENT: Can I add to [Student 2's] idea?
LINDSAY: Of course. [observation debrief]

Lindsay continued to position students as capable of working on science ideas and directing the science practice. For example, Lindsay, when visiting a small group discussion, reminded students that they are intellectuals capable of engaging in science practice. Note how Lindsay presses students to engage in epistemic work and not merely to repeat information.

LINDSAY, *to group*: Tell me why Marfan's syndrome occurs. And tell me how it's similar to your disorder. Paul [a student], what's yours?

PAUL: Similar because it's deletion.

LINDSAY: Where does it happen?

PAUL: In your DNA.

LINDSAY: But where?

PAUL: In amino acids?

LINDSAY: Talk as a group. Paul said that Marfan's and hemophilia are deletion.

Where do they occur?

STUDENT 2: Mutations occur in DNA. It's at a certain number.

LINDSAY: Oh, right. You all found a map of a chromosome on the internet. Why do mutations matter?

STUDENT 2: Because it changes DNA of future cells.

LINDSAY: OKAY.

STUDENT 2: Changes nucleotide, which cause change in gene, which causes change in protein.

LINDSAY: Okay, but what about . . .

STUDENT 3 [injects]: RNA.

LINDSAY: Okay. Great idea.

STUDENT 3: It has to turn into RNA to get codons to get amino acid.

LINDSAY: I think you're saying that it's complicated. Where in the process do mutations occur?

STUDENT 2: For sure.

PAUL: Hmmm . . . we didn't think that all the way through.

STUDENT 3: Can we work on it now?

LINDSAY: Of course.

At the end of this episode, students did not arrive at a final answer, and Lindsay allowed them to continue theorizing as a group. The lack of an answer may seem scary and uncertain, but Lindsay recognized that scientists—and students—need time and space to think about and discuss explanations.

Importantly, Lindsay's persistent use of talk moves that purposefully positioned students as important thinkers set a foundational tone for the classroom community's growth. Students began to see and hear different possibilities for their participation and, over time, began to trust that their talk was valued.

Anna's students, also supported to share their ideas and experiences, reported similar realizations about the importance of their participation. For example, one student in Anna's class noted, "In my other classes, we are not allowed to talk. We just have to be right. But here, it's like I'm supposed to try out what I think, and I'm supposed to help others think too." This student captures the shift in classroom culture that Lindsay and Anna hoped to initiate. Subsequently, students began making public discursive moves that promoted *their* ideas as important for the classroom science practice community. For example, students began to assign value to science ideas—including their peers' science ideas—and began to trust that Lindsay and Anna wanted to hear their thinking. Rather than shutting down such talk, Lindsay and Anna encouraged students to question and probe each other's thinking, as well as to problematize the textbook explanation for a phenomenon.

Take a moment to contrast the words of Lindsay and Anna with a different path of talk found in many classrooms, such as Teacher A's (see the introduction). While Lindsay and Anna purposefully and publicly placed value on students' thinking and positioned them as people who should shape science practices, other teachers might maintain the power to shape science practice by positioning students as passive receivers of information whose role is to reproduce canonical science ideas. In such classrooms, students must receive permission to talk on the public plane about science ideas. When allowed to speak, students typically state answers they think are correct and only ask questions to clarify instructions of the teacher. Given the classroom culture in these schools, students rarely, if ever, use talk moves similar to those found in Lindsay's and Anna's classrooms.

Given the difference between talk moves in Lindsay's and Anna's classrooms and the talk in classrooms of Teacher A and others, I created a table to help describe different types of interactions. Interestingly, I found that many of us use similar categories of talk moves when we interact with students. The difference, as we have seen with Lindsay and Anna, is whether we recognize points of departure and choose to place value on student thinking. Thus, table 4.1 gives examples of ways in which we can open up opportunities for students to help create a classroom community or narrow how we want students to participate and produce what we think are correct answers.

TABLE 4.1 **Educators' talk moves to open up participation or perpetuate epistemic injustice**

Talk moves	Examples from classrooms to open up participatory opportunities	Examples from classrooms that perpetuate epistemic injustice
Inquire about students' science ideas: A public statement about the knowledge status of a science idea	Teachers asked each other for evidence or ideas to support or refute prior statements: "How do you know that?" "What is your evidence?" "Unpack that claim some more."	Teachers asked students about the "correctness" of ideas: "What is wrong with what you just said?" "How can we fix [a student's] wrong answer?"
Question: A public question about an idea or a question designed to prompt idea sharing or emergence	*Clarify* (asking students to unpack their thinking): "What do you mean? Please tell me more about your idea." *Soliciting information* (genuine desire to understand situation better): "[Student], you just told the class about your experience going in a sauna after a cold swim. Could you please go a bit further—what did you notice about your shivering that seemed to connect with homeostasis?" *Participation* (encouraging sharing ideas on public plane): "I want to know all of your ideas. If you are not comfortable sharing out loud, write down your hypothesis on a piece of paper and turn it in. I want to see everyone's thoughts." *Metacognitive* (why are you doing this?): "How does what you said just now relate to our model, activity, or current idea thread?" (When student says something tangential, she does not dismiss it.) Also: "I want you to be aware of how your thinking is changing over time."	*Clarify* (used to diagnose misconceptions): "What do you mean? Do you really mean something else?" *Soliciting information* (asking a question to have students align with a teacher's way of seeing the world): "How many of you have ever seen identical twins?" *Demanding student participation*: "Can you please to pay attention so we can finish this practice problem?" *Rhetorical* (a question posed typically at the end of discussion that is never again addressed): "How could a fertilized egg split to have twins? We're now left with that question until another day."

(continued)

TABLE 4.1 **Educators' talk moves to open up participation or perpetuate epistemic injustice** (*continued*)

Talk moves	Examples from classrooms to open up participatory opportunities	Examples from classrooms that perpetuate epistemic injustice
Signal: A public statement indicating how students and the teacher should participate in the classroom community.	*Participation* (general expectations for how to participate in class): "If you are finished, help others. We are all responsible for each other's learning." "When one person is sharing, everyone else is silent. We respect, listen, and consider all ideas in this class." *Quality of idea* (the value of an idea): "Do not worry about being correct—just worry about 'did I use evidence from my life or a class activity when I said what I said?'" "Your idea is very strong because you used your peers' hypotheses and tried to tie them together." *Ascribing ownership of ideas* (Using students' ideas as resources during class time): "Michael has this hypothesis, so we will call it 'Michael's hypothesis,' and I will write it on the board so we can test it." *Ascribing expertise to students* (teacher telling students they can think and act like a scientist): "We are testing your ideas, not mine." "This is your time to reason and make claims; you can do it." "The local government scientists need your help—you know things they do not."	*Participation in classroom and/or science community* (general expectations for how to participate in class): "It is silent time to work on your own ideas; be sure to tell me when you are finished so I can check your work." *Quality of idea* (the value of an idea): "That is correct." "Nope, try again." *Ascribing ownership of ideas* (using students' ideas as resources during class time): "Did everyone see how Jonas said that? That's the way your explanation should sound." *Ascribing expertise to resources*: "Let's now look at the textbook's answers to fix our mistakes." "That was great talking in small groups. Take out paper to copy down the right answer from these PowerPoint notes."
Publicize private ideas: Teachers publicly and purposefully telling students ideas or actions that may be invisible to students.	*Revoicing* (teachers or students publicly restate a science idea): "Here's what I heard you say [repeats student's science idea]. What do other people think?"	*Revoicing* (teacher repeats student's science idea to gauge the "correctness" of the idea): "I think I heard you saying that the more acceleration something has, the more force it has?" Student: "Yes." Teacher: "That's true."

Talk moves	Examples from classrooms to open up participatory opportunities	Examples from classrooms that perpetuate epistemic injustice
Publicize private ideas (*continued*)	*Summarizing* (teachers or students repeat several science ideas in relation to a science activity): "Let's take a second and see where we are because we have three ideas in play right now. Robert claims that when potential energy goes down, kinetic energy goes up. Shuana agrees, but she is wondering about the role of friction in this possible relationship. Tran is hypothesizing that if we move the starting point of the roller coaster higher the kinetic energy will increase and will decrease friction's force." *Reasoning* (pedagogical and scientific—teacher explains why they engage in certain actions or answered a question in a particular way): "We are doing this summary table because we need to organize our activities and see what evidence we have, and because we need to make claims using evidence; we cannot just say this is 'just because.' The summary table helps us link evidence to parts of our explanatory model."	*Summarizing* (teacher stitches together students' science ideas to construct correct answer): "I'm going to take all of the ideas I've heard and put them together for the correct answer."
Instructions: How to begin and complete a task, routine, or discussion. Often include participatory norms.	"You have five minutes to finish writing your hypothesis and then discuss it with your partner. Remember to use evidence when talking to each other and ask each other questions if you don't understand your partner's hypothesis."	"You have five minutes to complete the writing assignment. Be sure to make your paragraph five sentences long. You are required to turn this in at the end of class."
Tagging on: Teacher or student injects facts or information to a conversation.	Student: "The average body temperature is 97 degrees." Teacher: "Actually it's 98.6 degrees. But your statement begs two questions. First, what does 'average body temperature' mean? Two, why is it 98.6 degrees and not 97 degrees?"	Student: "Carbon has four valence electrons." Teacher: "Because it already has two electrons in the inner shell."

(continued)

TABLE 4.1 **Educators' talk moves to open up participation or perpetuate epistemic injustice** (*continued*)

Talk moves	Examples from classrooms to open up participatory opportunities	Examples from classrooms that perpetuate epistemic injustice
Push or pull ideas: Dismissing (pushing) or extracting (pulling) students' science ideas during discussion.	*Pulling ideas:* "I see that no one wants to share their ideas right now. That's fine. There is a lot to think about. I do want to know about your thinking at this point of the unit, so let's take 5 minutes and you can write silently, with a partner, or you can come talk with me in our idea space [back corner of the classroom] about what we should do next."	*Pulling ideas:* Teacher: "Where is DNA?" Student: "In a cell." Teacher: "Where?" Student: "Inside." Teacher: "Where?" Student: "In the nucleus." Teacher: "Good." *Pushing ideas:* Student: "Why do some parents have triplets?" Teacher: "That doesn't have to do with our conversation about twins right now." Student: "What about valence electrons of middle elements?" Teacher: "We might get to those next week."
"Move on" moments: Teacher cuts off conversation or idea sharing for the purpose of advancing through an agenda, schedule, or curriculum.	*Providing space for "tangential" talk* (teacher lets student ask question or share their idea and provides them with a way to keep idea in play): Student: "I heard that astronauts say going up in a rocket is like a roller coaster. Is that true?" Teacher: "That is an interesting idea. We don't have time to talk about it right now, but if you write it down and put it in our class 'parking lot' [a poster used for students to write down any question or idea they have about science], I or another student will answer it before the unit is over."	*Refocusing "tangential" talk* (teacher lets students talk about ideas related to topic, but then refocuses student thinking): Teacher [after hearing students' science ideas]: "I want to rein you back in." *Cutting off ideas* (teacher abruptly stops student from discussing their idea further in public): Student: "How do scientists know that alleles are alleles?" Teacher: "That's enough of that. We need to move on."

Whenever I reflect on the talk moves that teachers have make in classrooms, I find three important themes that stand out when thinking with colleagues about classroom culture.

Theme 1: *Trust.* Lindsay, Anna, and many other teachers work with students to establish mutual trust. The process of trusting other people as capable, smart, and important to the classroom community can be slow, but the work is crucial. Historians and sociologists who study science cultures have learned that trust between people is critical for creating science knowledge and practices, and that this trust is slowly developed over time.[3] Once people in a setting see each other as trustworthy, they are more willing to engage in novel and interesting science work.

Theme 2: *Science is public.* Another purposeful instructional move by Lindsay, Anna, and other teachers is to position science as a public practice, making the class the collective "knower." By working to create communities in which everyone plays an important role in learning, teachers align with research conducted by historians and sociologists of science. For example, sociologist Karin Knorr-Cetina found that productive labs are places where "[l]ab leaders counteract and dissipate the individualizing forces and the social power accumulated by certain individuals and groups."[4] In other words, places in which epistemic injustice is disrupted are classrooms and schools where the community, not the individual, is working collectively on science. As we have seen in Lindsay's and Anna's classrooms, the teachers worked to make all students' science ideas important, and over time, the science work of the classroom became more student-driven. These classrooms run counter to the narrative of many American schools, which place value on individual success over collective inquiry.[5]

Theme 3: *Messiness.* While the image of science often depicted in schools is that knowledge is acquired through linear and straightforward processes, Lindsay's and Anna's classrooms embody the messiness of science. By messiness, I mean that science rarely unfolds as we plan and expect. As teachers with instructional authority, Lindsay and Anna had to make in-the-moment decisions that required, in some cases, recasting an entire unit of instruction around students' ideas, such as Lindsay's ivy unit. These rapid instructional adaptations led to the classroom science activity resembling what sociologist Andrew Pickering called the "mangle of practice." Given the unpredictability of contextual factors, Pickering argued, "[W]e do not know what other people, or even ourselves, will do next . . . The goals of scientific practice emerge in the real time of practice."[6] Lindsay and Anna show us through their talk moves that, rather than panicking when activities do not work or students veer in unplanned directions, we should emphasize to students that science often occurs in such fits and starts. Rather than orderly and objective, we can encourage students to embrace the messiness of science work; this stance is more authentic to how science occurs in the real world.

STUDENT TALK MOVES

Our talk moves, beginning on the first day of the school year, are crucially important to setting the participatory tone and for placing immediate value on student thinking. I can imagine that one question we might ask as we consider our talk moves might be: "If I use talk moves to open up opportunities for students to shape science, how will I know if students will actually participate?" In the next chapter, we will consider students' actions, especially as they help shape the science practices and activities in a classroom. For now, we will focus on students' talk moves as an indicator that they are moving beyond participation that prioritizes reciting correct answers.

Recall that Lindsay and Anna make purposeful and public statements beginning on the first day of school to help establish a powerful narrative about the importance of students and their ideas. However, Lindsay and Anna would be the first people to tell you that the process of building trust—especially about talk—takes time. Initially, students may be quite skeptical about whether you actually want to hear their thinking and care about their cultural experiences. Such skepticism is justified. Consider how often schools tell students that their ideas and experiences are not valuable—the core of epistemic injustice. Thus, students may need weeks or months of coherent experiences in your classroom and school before they trust that you care about them as people. Lindsay and Anna would also tell you that this relational work of establishing trust is the foundation of equitable teaching.

Over time, the process of codeveloping a classroom community may become evident in students' talk moves. Table 4.2 describes different kinds of talk moves that I heard students make in Lindsay's and Anna's classrooms.

TABLE 4.2. **Examples of students' discursive moves illustrating epistemic agency**

Discursive move made by students	Example from classroom observations
Making claims (students asserted science ideas in relation to phenomenon under study)	*About knowledge or data*: "I think that the roller coaster energy decreases because it gets slower at the bottom of the loop."
	"I think that our data shows that our body is trying to counteract the increase in our temperature by cooling down the rest of our body."
	Agree or disagree with others: "I agree with Michael's hypothesis because in our roller coaster model, the marble needed to increase speed to get through the loop" (Anna's class). "I disagree with Sean because I do not think that our brain can control how fast electric impulses travel across neurons."
	Invoking evidence: "Our data shows that the speed of the roller coaster decreases constantly as it goes up a ramp."
	Explanation talk: "Maybe our homeostatic responses are related—there could be a relationship between the increase in heart rate, breathing rate, and temperature."
Integrated science ideas with other ideas (students made sense of their science ideas with other science ideas brought up on the public plane)	*Personal experience*: "Once when I went downhill in my car, my dad didn't put on the brakes. We went so fast—faster and faster as we went further down the hill."
	Invoking other student and teacher ideas: "I want to add onto James's idea about temperature. He said that the brain controls how fast temperature increases. Perhaps also the brain controls *whether or not* temperature increases at all."
	Challenge science ideas: "I am not sure about that claim. Can you please talk about the activity that made you say that?"
	Predict: "When we exercise faster, our temperature will increase because we are burning energy faster."
	Propose tests or experiments: "To test the hypothesis about heart rate, let's do jumping jacks for one minute and then immediately take our temperature—we can do it several times and see if our temperature increases when heart rate increases."

(continued)

TABLE 4.2. **Examples of students' discursive moves illustrating epistemic agency** (*continued*)

Discursive move made by students	Example from classroom observations
Question (students asked other students and the teacher about science ideas)	*Clarify*: "Are you saying that cells divide faster if they are cancerous?"
	Inquire about science ideas: "Can you explain more about what you mean by 'heat energy' (Anna's class)?"
Introduced new Science ideas to public plane (students elevated their own science ideas to the public plane they felt were missing from the community's discussion)	"Our roller coaster model is missing gravity—we haven't talked about that yet."
Assign value to ideas (students gave other student's science ideas value)	"I like your idea—you back it up with evidence."
	"Your idea will help our model become more explanatory."

As people with power, our words and actions send explicit and implicit messages to students about who is permitted to "do" science and who should have a voice in what counts as science. Efforts to restrict science to a single scientific method and textbook information often results in students thinking that science is a static set of procedures and facts that they reproduce on standardized assessments, and that usually White men (and a few White women) can become successful as scientists.[7] As we saw in Teacher A's classroom, students learn that their ideas, unless canonically correct, are unimportant. Subsequently, their participation in classroom science decreased.

By reimagining power structures and by purposefully elevating students' ideas as important, Lindsay and Anna work toward a classroom community in which science is a collaborative effort shaped by everyone in the room. Lindsay and Anna make their stance public through talk moves that happen frequently over time: students can and should become active producers of scientific knowledge rather than passively receive information about someone else's science. Our colleagues Beth Warren and Ann Rosebery refer to this stance as "equity in the future tense," in which teachers work to problematize the asymmetric disciplinary power structures between teachers and students. They note, "[W]e believe that the remaking of science education into a more egalitarian sense-making practice entails deep transformations of identity for teachers and students alike, transformations that empower them to think, talk, and act scientifically.[8] To undermine this power difference means that teachers and students together dismantle an entrenched message of science instruction and larger American society—that competition and individuality are the sole means to achieving scientific success.

As Anna and Lindsay illustrate, the most productive science classroom communities are the result of many individuals working in concert.[9] Rather than science, and society, becoming a hierarchy of cognitive authority in which technicians (i.e., students) and others are put in lower and *less powerful* positions, Lindsay and Anna show us how students should shape novel science classroom communities. Students in these communities learn that their ideas can and should have a bearing on the knowledge and practice that develop over time.

CONCLUDING ACTIVITIES

As we have seen in Lindsay's and Anna's classrooms, teachers have immense power to open up or constrain students' opportunities for participation. Using talk moves that value student thinking and position students as important "knowers" in the classroom, teachers and students can begin to create powerful classroom communities. Ideally, teachers and students should engage in purposeful talk with elaborating, questioning, and reorganizing of ideas as the goal; students' ideas are uncompromisingly treated as intellectual resources for everyone's learning.

To conclude this chapter, let's engage in a three-part exercise together to think about our talk moves as teachers and administrators, and how such talk moves open up or constrain opportunities for students to participate in the classroom community. Remember that while every exercise can be completed individually, our collective thinking and conversations will help advance everyone's classrooms and schools.

Part 1: Classroom and School Observations

Since this chapter focuses on classroom talk, and the power that talk and participation have in shaping a classroom community, we need to pay attention to what happens in classrooms and schools. We need to start listening to classroom and school talk through a lens of equity, and to consider how our talk moves and actions open up or constrain students' opportunities for participation.

For the first part of this activity, you can choose to visit a live classroom or school, or you can find videos of classrooms and schools online (for example, you can go to the video gallery of the Ambitious Science Teaching website or the Third International Mathematics and Science Study [TIMSS] 1999 Video Study).[10] When you watch the classrooms and schools (in person or on video), be sure to make observations about:

- *Who* is talking and participating
- *When* people talk and participate
- *What kind of* talk and participation is permitted
- *How* certain talk and participation are *supported*

Part 2: Classroom Reflections

Now that you have observed some classrooms through the lens of talk moves, spend time reflecting on what you watched. Before diving into the questions, remember that your conversation should honor the teachers or administrators, students, and spaces you viewed. Avoid blame and "repair talk"—making suggestions about what the teacher should have done in a moment—because judgment is easy when you are not the person in the classroom or school. You will have a productive conversation if you think about the talk moves teachers and students made, and how those talk moves support further participation or close down avenues for students. As teachers and administrators, we are always learning. We must remember that everyone is on a learning journey, and together, we can help each other grow to better support students.

For this second part, let's consider our observation notes and talk with each other about these questions:

- What do you notice about who is talking and how they are talking?
- Why might differences in talk exist in the classroom and school?
- Did you notice any talk moves by a teacher, administrator, or student that send a signal about talk?

Part 3: Next Steps

Finally, after thinking about the classroom and school observations, we need to plan some concrete steps to reimagine our communities. In part 3, we reflect on our evolving thinking and make commitments about actions we will take in the upcoming days, weeks, and years to shift opportunities for student talk and participation. Let's consider:

- What insights into student thinking, talk, and participation are you considering after the observations? What are some new ideas that you are considering about student thinking, talk, and participation? What sparked these ideas for you?
- How will you use your insights into student thinking, talk, and participation to make some choices about teaching next week? What will you do during the upcoming week in response to something you learned about students' thinking, talk, and participation?
- How might you collect some data about student learning and participation given your plan?

FIVE

Making Knowledge Production Practices Visible and Shaped by Students

IN CHAPTER 4, we focused on the talk moves that teachers and students develop and use to signify that ideas, experiences, and cultures are needed to shape the classroom community. Certainly, these talk moves—both in-the-moment interactions and a suite of talk moves built over time—are crucial for disrupting epistemic injustice in schools. However, talk moves alone will not create equitable classroom communities. Worse, a mismatch between equitable talk moves and inequitable learning opportunities becomes confusing for students and might seem that teachers and administrators do not really care about their ideas; instead, they are playing a game.

Consider an example. I observed Teacher C's classroom for weeks and noticed that they used talk moves similar to those we encountered in chapter 4 to open up possibilities for students. Students appreciated these opportunities, and I watched excellent conversations occur when students were in small groups and when the teacher was eliciting their initial ideas about a phenomenon. However, as a unit progressed, Teacher C became worried that students needed to acquire correct answers that might appear on the state science assessment. Teacher C still offered talk opportunities in small groups but started to conclude class by saying, "Great conversations today. Let me give you the correct answer." Initially, students were confused and asked why they could share any ideas in small groups but have those ideas discounted at the end of class. Teacher C responded that they could both talk about their ideas and receive the correct answer from the teacher. Rather than press Teacher C for further justification, the students collectively decided to refrain from talking in small groups because, as one student told me, "What's the point of talking if the teacher is just going to give us the right answer? [They] pretend like [they] want to hear my ideas, but [they] don't really care." Many students shared this sentiment, and subsequently, their participation in small groups decreased. Thus began a vicious cycle of mutual frustration: Teacher C noticed the participation change and began to publicly chastise students for their lack of conversation. In turn, students became less likely to talk about anything in the class, and over time, their participation dwindled (much like Teacher A's classroom) because they did not want to draw the ire of Teacher C.

Given this example, there are two important ideas that we will consider in this chapter to build on our thinking in chapter 4. First, students want a teacher who cares about them and provides opportunities for their thinking to shape classroom actions. Students become justifiably frustrated when teachers and administrators insert their power to claim sole authority over the knowledge and practices in a classroom and school. Second, the words and actions of teachers and administrators must align. I think of this alignment as *coherence* between what we think, say, and do in classrooms and schools. Students will quickly realize if teachers and administrators pretend to listen to their thinking but have already developed a valued and predetermined participatory path that remains invisible to others.

In this chapter, we will link the talk moves that signal how we care about students to the pedagogical and science practices we enact and codevelop with students in classrooms and schools. We will think together about coherence between thoughts, words, and actions so that we can create profound classrooms in which students feel heard, seen, and valued as community members. In addition, we will think about the tools we can design with students to support our collective learning. As a reminder, this chapter will focus more on the pedagogical and science practices in classrooms, but such practices are inextricably linked with our talk moves (please revisit chapter 4 anytime).

Finally, as we consider science practices and teaching practices that build strong classroom communities, we also need to be explicit about how our teaching and interactions with students aim to disrupt epistemic injustice and create equitable opportunities. Our friends and colleagues Megan Bang, Bryan Brown, Angela Calabrese Barton, Ann Rosebery, and Beth Warren describe three important principles about equitable science education for us to remember as we plan, teach, and reflect:

1. See and value students' ways of sensemaking, and honor those ways as scientific.
2. Place students' sensemaking as a foundational part of classrooms and purposefully provide opportunities for such sensemaking to drive the work of the community.
3. Honor and recognize the multitude of community and cultural practices that students use to understand the world and provide opportunities to put such practices in conversation with each other to create a more expansive view of science.[1]

These principles help us remember that all students can and should contribute to the science work of our classroom communities, and that our primary job as teachers and administrators is to help students feel safe to think and share ideas.

SCIENCE PRACTICES

To begin thinking about coherence between our talk moves and students' learning opportunities, let's reflect again about the science of our classrooms and schools. More specifically, we should consider the word "practice," and how that very popular word is related to our classroom communities. As you know, the term "science practice" occupies significant airtime in conversations about science classrooms, especially when we talk about the Next Generation Science Standards (NGSS). You have likely heard that the NGSS are supposed to help us reframe students' learning expectations around participation in science practices.[2] I am also guessing that you have encountered a surge in new resources (i.e., curricula, textbooks, kits) claiming to help you provide science practice opportunities for students in your classrooms and schools.

While I am glad that we are collectively thinking about science practices as important, there are two unresolved issues about practice that can potentially limit the impact of our work. First, "science practice" can be a vague term. While we agree that students should engage in authentic science activities, there is little consensus about the specific dimensions of disciplinary work that students should learn. Second, establishing a definition of science practice does not automatically result in opportunities for students to engage in such work. Many factors, including people (e.g., teachers and administrators) and resources (e.g., curricula and materials), play crucial roles in providing (or limiting) opportunities for students to learn science practice.

Given these two issues, I offer a definition of science practices, and then we will look at how this definition is related to our words and actions as teachers and administrators. I define science practice as the learnable and valued dimensions of disciplinary work, both tacit and explicit, that people develop over time in a specific place, such as a laboratory, field station, and classroom. To arrive at this definition, I use two overlapping perspectives about *practice*—the dimensions of disciplinary work and descriptions of how novices learn to participate in valued community activities. Combined, the dual components of this definition imply that learning science practice involves a reframing of teaching and learning expectations away from the memorization of information to engagement in disciplinary work.

Dimensions of Disciplinary Work

When we think about learning science in schools, we often think about science knowledge as the main objective for students. While science knowledge can be important, there are other dimensions of science that are often left unmentioned or kept invisible to students:

- *A conceptual dimension.* How people use theories, principles, laws, and ideas to make sense of the world
- *A social dimension.* How people agree on norms and routines for handling, developing, critiquing, and using ideas
- *An epistemic dimension.* The philosophical basis by which people decide what they know and why they are believe ideas to be true
- *A material dimension.* How people create, adapt, and use tools, technologies, and other resources to support their intellectual work[3]

These four dimensions of disciplinary work can help us remember that science is not created in solitude by a genius in a laboratory. Instead, science practice emerges from a larger network of activity that includes specialized discourse and historical norms for participation, and is influenced by social, political, and cultural aspects of a context.[4]

Learning to Participate in Disciplinary Work

While labeling the four dimensions of practice is useful for naming parts of science that are often hidden from students, such labeling does not describe how practice can imply the learning of professional disciplinary work. To better describe practice as learning, our friend and colleague Magdalene Lampert offers three descriptions of the term "practice," which we can apply to thinking about science learning and classroom communities.[5] First, practice is thought of in a global sense—the practice of science. This perspective means that students develop a vision about what scientists do and construct an identity as a scientist over time, taking on and adapting common values, language, and disciplinary tools. Second, science practice can describe a collection of practices. Students, then, learn to participate in, and challenge, the valued daily work of scientists. Third, science practice involves the opportunities for students to rehearse daily routines and to receive feedback about how their efforts to engage in science are progressing.

As we know, opportunities for students to learn science practice, as defined, are rare. Therefore, classroom communities around science practice requires a fundamental shift in the priorities of teaching and learning. Merely exposing students to definitions of science practice, or having students complete activities of which the sole purpose is to confirm canonical information, is not the same as providing opportunities for students to learn science practice by engaging in authentic disciplinary work over time.

Themes About Science Practice from Science Studies

Scholars in other fields (such as historians and philosophers of science) can help us better understand how we might better support students' learning opportunities. Here, let's look at three themes from science studies literature to think about implications for our classrooms and schools.

Theme 1: *Whose science practice?* A first important question to ask about the science practice that students learn is: *Whose practice?* To expand the question, philosopher Sandra Harding asks, "Whose agendas does and should science pursue? Whose hypotheses, concepts, preferred research designs, preferred understandings of nature, social relations, and inquiry should be supported?"[6] Such questions may initially seem nonsensical; science practice is often presented as unaffected by the values and interests of its context.[7] However, science practice is inherently bound to a community—scientists and learners engage in the work valued and promoted by their particular set of contextual circumstances.

Linking the development of disciplinary work to contextual circumstances problematizes the view of science promoted in many learning settings, that *all* sciences share *a* universal practice, often called "the scientific method," or that there is a single "nature of science," that students should learn. However, many science educators have pushed to discard the scientific method and the nature of science because they misconstrue how science practice develops in the real world.[8] By discarding the assumption of a universal science practice, however, a new conundrum emerges: Whose science practice should be privileged in learning settings? I propose two interpretations of this question.

First, each science community engages in unique forms of practice. For example, microbiologists and cosmologists can both claim science as their overarching discipline, but the standards for practice (for example, how evidence is evaluated and used) differ. Therefore, the community in which science develops shapes the features of the disciplinary practice that novices are permitted to learn.

Subject-specific practice differences have implications for teaching and learning across settings. For example, our friend and colleague Ron Gray notes that most inquiry experiences in secondary science classrooms are heavily weighted toward experimentation, while many fields of science (e.g., evolutionary biology, cosmology, and paleontology) are not necessarily justified by experimental methodologies.[9] Therefore, a teacher's or curriculum's focus on experimentation could limit particular forms of science practice in classrooms.

A second interpretation of "whose science practice" is to consider disciplinary work from the perspective of power and authority. Science studies scholars argue that *who* is theorizing matters for the practice develops over time. Typically, a division exists between those permitted to create and certify science practice and those without authority who are typically assigned the tasks that those with power deem necessary. These divisions result in a hierarchy in which those without authority are placed in *less powerful* positions.[10] Kathryn Addelson suggests that such divisions in power have a bearing on "what counts" as acceptable science practice, how newcomers are trained, and how measures and methods are standardized.[11]

Rather than engage in science practice as determined by those with power, some science studies scholars press for "science from below" in which disciplinary practice is initiated by those typically excluded from such work.[12] In science education, our friends and colleagues Doug Medin and Megan Bang offer an example by describing the development of ecologically oriented and community-based science education programs, both of which promote non-privileged cultural groups' knowledge-making practices.[13] Thus an answer to "whose science practice" can include opportunities for students to codevelop and legitimately participate in disciplinary work.

Theme 2: *Science as a public or private practice.* A second theme in science practice is whether disciplinary work is framed as public or private. Often, science is portrayed as a private practice in which lone scientists discover truths about the world that they later reveal to the broader public. Other scholars, however, argue that science is inherently a public practice in which communities are more productive because they consist of many individuals working in concert.[14] Thus, public interactions of actors, tools, resources, and historical norms in a context shape, and are shaped by, developing science practice.

However, many learning settings uphold science as a private practice by positioning individual students as responsible for their own learning and success as scientists. In these settings, educators tacitly (or explicitly) hide students' ideas, experiences, and expertise from other students. To counteract the privatization of science, some teachers purposefully position science as a public practice in which students and teachers codevelop ideas, models, methodologies, and explanations.

Theme 3: *How science practice develops and unfolds over time.* A third theme in science practice is the manner in which practice develops and unfolds over time. As previously mentioned, most science learning settings promote the scientific method as the norm for disciplinary work. According to the scientific method, scientists conduct "fair test" experiments to test variables in a linear fashion, thus confirming canonical information.[15]

Instead of the linear and controlled version of science, science studies scholars offer a different image of science practice in which disciplinary work is constantly reinvented given emerging circumstances, despite practitioners' best efforts to plan meticulously before beginning their work.[16] Portraying science practice as constantly adapting to contextual circumstances aligns with Andrew Pickering's concept of the "mangle of practice," in which "the goals of scientific practice emerge in the real time of practice."[17] Therefore, having students learn that science is a linear testing of single variables does not represent how science practice actually develops.

As the three themes from science studies literature illuminate, promoting science as a constantly evolving set of value-laden public routines in which students can (and should) take an active role in developing requires science educators to reframe the work of teaching and learning across settings.

TEACHING PRACTICES

Thinking deeply about science practices is part of the important work we must do to reimagine classrooms and disrupt epistemic injustice. However, the science practices of a classroom are closely linked with the teaching practices that are enacted and valued in classrooms and schools. Here, we will think together about teaching practices and how those are linked to science practices. Next, we will examine some examples from Lindsay's and Anna's classrooms in which teaching and science practices are negotiated with students. While we will think generally about teaching practices, if you are interested in taking a deeper dive into teaching practices and tools to support equitable learning opportunities, I recommend the book *Ambitious Science Teaching* by our friends and colleagues Mark Windschitl, Jessica Thompson, and Melissa Braaten.[18]

As we see in Lindsay's and Anna's classrooms, spaces for equitable learning opportunities that disrupt epistemic injustice do not occur naturally, do not materialize because of luck, and do not instantly appear the moment students walk into a building. As teachers and administrators, we must help create spaces and opportunities for students, and therefore we should consider how our role in classrooms and schools aligns with equitable science practices goals.

My stance, along with our friend and colleague Mark Windschitl, is that our primary instructional task is to provide opportunities for all students to participate in science as a knowledge-building enterprise that focuses on developing important ideas in the discipline and ideas that are meaningful to them.[19] We caution that teachers and administrators—not curricula, standards, or assessments—are the key to reimagining classrooms. While curricula, standards, and assessments can be useful, an exclusive focus on those documents may result in a checkoff system for addressing performance expectations one by one during units of instruction. Such teaching does not fundamentally change the learning environment for students because they do not utilize the research base that describes how students actually learn to engage in, and shape, disciplinary work. Instead, we offer four principles for teaching practice that, seen through lenses of equity, can help create powerful classroom communities. Importantly, the four principles are interdependent, meaning that none of the conditions or experiences expressed in them support learning without being used in conjunction with others.

Principle 1: Teachers Provide Varied Opportunities for Students to Reason Through Talk

This principle builds on the ideas of chapter 4, which focus on talk moves between teachers and students. Importantly, we can design opportunities for powerful talk in individual lessons and over the school year. Across disciplines and theories of learning, we know that student learning is greatly enhanced when we provide structured opportunities to talk about science and by orchestrating powerful conversations between students. From our perspective of disrupting epistemic injustice, the talk moves that we facilitate, such as asking classmates to compare their ideas, encouraging students to unpack their reasoning in a supportive environment, and allowing them to comment on their current state of understanding, has led to deeper engagement in the content and to participation by students who would otherwise remain on the margins of classroom activity.[20] As teachers and administrators, we can establish and maintain norms for civil conversations, deploy a repertoire of discourse strategies that can stimulate productive forms of student talk, represent and rehearse disciplinary-specific ways of using language with students, and support students talking to each other without an adult monitoring every conversation.[21]

Principle 2. Treating Students' Ideas and Experiences as Resources to Build on

As teacher and administrators, we know that when students link their current understanding and experiences to new ideas, powerful learning can occur. When we think about creating equitable classroom communities, we must center students' cultural, experiential, and cognitive resources as crucial to everyone's learning. Teachers and administrators play a crucial role in helping students apply their existing resources to the work of the classroom community. Skilled teachers and administrators use instructional practices and tools that elicit these potential resources and help elevate student ideas for public discussion.[22] For example, as we've seen in Anna's and Lindsay's classrooms, when teachers use students' initial explanations and everyday experiences as resources, students are more likely to collaboratively revise and consolidate their ideas through participation in science discussions. As Anna and Lindsay enact such opportunities, students feel more welcomed as scientists and as smart people with important ideas.

Principle 3. Student Thinking Is Routinely Made Public for the Classroom Community

When thinking is made visible and elevated to the public plane of interaction in supportive classrooms, students' have powerful opportunities to learn with and from each other about science. As teachers and administrators, we play a central role in publicizing student thinking, such as their models, claims, rough draft explanations, hypotheses, and other inscriptions that the class then treats as objects of inquiry and revision. Students are positioned as an audience for each other's work and receive the necessary scaffolding to help one another shift ideas in light of new evidence, to rethink plans for investigations, or to clarify analogies they had developed to understand concepts. Students might do a peer review of classmates' written summaries about the implications of a recent experiment, participate in research meetings in which they converse about the benefits and limitations of different models for the same scientific phenomenon, or use representations of what they currently know about a phenomenon to generate new investigative questions.[23] These activities and conversations also make knowledge, modes of reasoning, academic language, and epistemic values available to all learners in the classroom. Such knowledge is sharable and indispensable to students for growing a classroom community. To make this possible, teachers codevelop with students the language and conventions for representing ideas, set standards together for what counts as reasons to change claims or ideas, and set norms for students about commenting on one another's ideas.

Principle 4. Teachers Scaffold Students' Attempts at Science-Specific Forms of Writing, Talk, and Participation in Activity

Scaffolding refers to the types of assistance that students receive to engage in work that is currently novel and difficult. Successful scaffolding strategies have taken a variety of forms, including reducing extraneous information in texts, introducing specialized intellectual roles for students in doing group work, making features of scientific work and expert thinking explicit to students, creating situations in which multilingual students can leverage their linguistic resources, and prompts to select from particular strategies to represent data to others.[24] Outcomes from studies about scaffolding have helped the research community recalibrate estimations of what learners can do with purposeful help. The implication for teachers and administrators is that we must develop a deep and flexible understanding of scaffolding given that nonroutine tasks will be ubiquitous in our classroom communities.

Taken together, these four principles, when aligned with goals for science practice, illustrate the importance of our role as teachers and administrators in providing opportunities for equitable science communities.

Teachers and Students Codeveloping Science Communities

Now that we are actively thinking about coherence of our thoughts, talk, and actions (for both science and teaching practices), let's look at more examples from Anna's and Lindsay's classrooms to see how they purposefully provided opportunities to codevelop science communities with students. By codevelop, I mean that teachers and students work together to decide on the participatory norms for science and as people in the physical space, and constantly revisit and revise the norms over time. As people with power in classrooms and schools, we must take an active stance in the codevelopment of practices and communities. We must provide opportunities for students to shape science rather than merely serve as passive participants in someone else's science, and we must make this stance public to students.

Let's now dive into Anna's and Lindsay's classrooms to see some examples of how they actively and publicly worked to codevelop communities with students through coherence of their emerging vision of equitable teaching, their talk moves, their pedagogical actions, and through tools they use, design, and adapt.

To support students' codeveloping of science communities, Anna purposefully used materials in the classroom to support students' participation. For example, in one lesson during the energy transformations unit, students recorded their ideas and attached them to a large drawing of a roller coaster taped to a classroom wall. One student, James, examined a peer's claim about energy on a sticky note. He disagreed with the claim, and Anna asked the other student, Ophelia, to walk over to the poster. In the conversation, Anna initially participated but then listened as the students discussed their ideas using the poster on the wall as a conceptual and epistemic anchor:

> ANNA, *pointing to the poster:* James, I want to know more about the amount of energy that the roller coaster has, like that you give it when you pull it up to this height versus this height.
>
> JAMES, *tracing the roller coaster track drawing with his finger:* So we pull it up [the car] to this height and give it a certain amount of energy.
>
> ANNA: How come it would go flying off the end?
>
> JAMES: 'Cause it still has something left.
>
> ANNA: So has it [the car] lost any energy?
>
> JAMES: Yeah, it [the car] lost a little bit.
>
> ANNA: A little bit but it hasn't lost enough.
>
> JAMES: But not enough to stop up here (*points to end of roller coaster track on poster*) and then even if it did stop up here, it wouldn't be able to go again (*looks at another student's sticky note on the poster*). But who thinks that with all that friction, it can still go back through?

ANNA, *looking at sticky note*: This is Ophelia's. Ophelia, can you come up here? James has a question for you.

[Ophelia walks from her table to the poster on the wall.]

JAMES, *to Ophelia*: Why did you say that the car can go through?

OPHELIA: I put the sticky note there because I thought the friction here (*points to drawing of roller coaster*) was not enough to stop the car.

JAMES: How about here where the track is high (*points to the roller coaster track*)?

OPHELIA: I think this side's a little better for the car, and so when it goes on the other side (*points to another part of the roller coaster track*), there is still energy for it to go again.

JAMES: It's not like it's just getting energy.

OPHELIA: I think that's the point, yeah, because it's (*points to the car on the poster*) still got energy left.

ANNA: So how have you resolved this?

JAMES: Now I know why she wrote it.

Note that the students both used the poster—tracing the energy with their finger—when describing their idea. By placing the poster on the wall for public use, Anna provided an opportunity for students to examine, evaluate, and discuss each other's ideas; in other words, Anna's use of posters and wall space provided opportunities for students to tinker with a model.

In another example, Anna created an "idea space" in the classroom. Anna conceived of the idea space when planning before the start of school. She assumed that students would "think that they can only be right or wrong, so I need to make a safe spot in the classroom where they can just think out loud. Hopefully that spills over into the rest of the classroom." Note that Anna purposefully designated a specific section in the classroom to have a particular meaning—a safe spot—in order to promote certain forms of engagement.

To move to the idea space, students carried their chairs to the back of the room. Anna and her students negotiated that the idea space was not a place for right answers; rather, students "know when they're back there that it doesn't matter if they are 'right,' I'm [Anna] going to write it down. That there's no wrong answer." In the idea space, students discussed theories, partial understandings of concepts, and observations from activities. During discussions,

Anna inscribed students' science ideas on a poster, which she then hung on a wall.

Returning to the roller coaster example, Anna wrote students' initial hypotheses about why the roller coaster car does not fly off the track after a long hill. Some students thought that the car "had more potential energy, and therefore has energy to use to keep it on the track." Other students hypothesized that the car "has more kinetic energy, and it counteracts the force of gravity to stay on the track." Thus Anna set up the idea space for a specific kind of interaction—students could tinker with ideas, record ideas on posters, and revisit the ideas over time.

In a similar way, Lindsay created purposeful opportunities for students to codesign science practices and a community. To think about some examples, let's revisit Lindsay's English ivy unit example. Like Anna, Lindsay encouraged students to use large poster paper to create representations of their thinking as they moved around the classroom. These representations acted as visual and conceptual anchors for the students' constantly evolving ideas. For example, after returning to their classroom with plant samples, Lindsay and her students constructed a list of seven hypotheses about why English ivy could be successfully outcompeting native plants in the students' community. This list remained on public display, taped to a classroom wall, throughout the unit. Student groups volunteered to test each of the seven separate hypotheses. Before running the actual experiments, students conducted a peer review of other groups' proposed experimental designs to ensure that the data from the experiment would provide evidence for the explanatory model and would not be the result of errors in the experimental design.

Second, Lindsay allowed students to use equipment to test hypotheses after they designed an experiment and consulted with each other about the procedure. As students planned and engaged in cycles of experimental work, they had permission to freely use laboratory equipment stationed at the back of the room—for example, a fume hood, microscopes, hot plates, water, and heat lamps. The experimental results fueled further rounds of model revisions, hypothesis generation, more trips out to the field to collect more samples, and discussions between students and Lindsay about their overarching explanation for the English ivy's success. Thus, the materials—representations of student thinking and equipment—promoted Lindsay's view that "messy" science required accessible and malleable materials that could be used in a nonlinear time frame.

In order for students to engage in messy work, Lindsay used her classroom to promote two features of science. First, Lindsay's classroom provided a safe place for students to publicly share and revise ideas without fear that their ideas might be dismissed. Often, Lindsay invoked the classroom as a safe place when making public statements about the constant generation and revising of hypotheses. For example, a common discursive exchange between Lindsay and her students often involved disrupting the notion of right or wrong answers:

STUDENT: I know we set up the experiment to test our idea [that ivy blocks out sunlight from other plants], but what if it's wrong?

LINDSAY: What do you mean by "wrong"?

STUDENT: What if blocking sunlight is not important? Then we just wasted everyone's time.

LINDSAY: Look around you at your ideas on the wall (*pointing to the representations of student thinking*). This is how messy science works. Sometimes hypotheses help explain a phenomenon. Sometimes hypotheses help revise our ideas by telling us what is not a part of the explanation. If your experiment shows that blocking sun is not a reason for the ivy's success, then we can still revise our posters based on your important finding.

Note that Lindsay tells the student that the classroom walls, which hold representations of student thinking, are sites that help students compile evidence to generate explanations. Lindsay deflects the student's worry—that they might get the wrong answer—and instead makes the sharing and recording of ideas the norm for participation.

A second feature of Lindsay's classroom was that science was a community endeavor. Lindsay wanted her classroom to enable students to "participate as scientists in a knowledge-making community because that's how scientists make sense of their back-and-forth work of testing and revising ideas." Such community work required that she design her classroom to allow collaboration between students. Lindsay, therefore, purposefully placed students in groups rather than have them sit individually. She also allowed students to move between groups when discussing ideas, creating space for students to easily walk back and forth between tables. For example, if different groups converged on similar ideas, Lindsay asked the groups to meet and discuss their findings. In addition, during designated times, students could freely move back and forth between tables, comparing models and hypotheses with other groups. Thus, Lindsay's classroom provided students with opportunities to engage in messy science work across sites.

Linking words and actions. Looking at Anna's and Lindsay's classes, there are three important ways that they linked science practices, teaching practices, and their words about equitable science communities. First, Anna and Lindsay codeveloped classrooms with students in which theories, models, and students' ideas constantly interacted across space and time. In addition, Anna and Lindsay framed science as public endeavor by permitting students to take their ideas and walk freely to other groups. Second, Anna and Lindsay used materials as resources to support different paths of theory testing and model development. Note that each participant's definition of science permeated the purpose of materials and the ways in which students used materials in the classroom. Even the use of wall space—placing different representations of science and students' ideas—conveyed specific messages about the collaborative practices of science. Third, Anna and Lindsay helped students take on the role of active and authentic participants in public science using pedagogical practices and tools. They encouraged students to use physical space, and each other, to actively engage in complex science practices that the community codeveloped.

CONCLUDING ACTIVITIES

Moving forward, let's think together about three aspects of our work around science practices, teaching practices, and codeveloping classrooms with students. As always, engaging in thinking and writing with colleagues helps us learn with and from each other.

Part 1: Initial Questions

To begin, let's think together about our classrooms in terms of science practices and teaching practices, and how we might codevelop science communities with students. For this part, let's consider both a generic classroom and classrooms in our schools. With colleagues, consider the following questions:

- In your classroom community, what counts as science knowledge and why? How do you know?
- What counts as science problems worth solving? Who decides and why?
- How do you recognize and resolve disagreements about emerging ideas?
- What opportunities exist to hear and build on students' ideas?
- What structures and opportunities currently exist that constrain or support students' participation?

As you consider these questions, think about your role in the classroom and school.

Part 2: Designing Tools

Given your answers to the initial questions, consider how Anna and Lindsay created, adapted, and used tools to help provide opportunities for students to codevelop science communities. For this part, you can consider tools to help with science teaching and learning.

First, let's consider the tasks you and students can design to name and investigate science phenomena. For this part, consider questions such as:

- What kinds of tasks do students want to enact, and why?
- Who gets to make decisions about the work involved, and how are roles assigned?
- What is the purpose of the task? How are tasks going to be used later in the lesson (or in future lessons)?

An important reminder for this task is that tasks should be complex and content-rich, and promote high expectations for student learning. Tasks should be designed in service of learning about big ideas and supporting students forming a collaborative community while engaged in complex thinking over time.

Second, let's design tools to help us record ideas, facilitate participation, and send messages about equitable learning opportunities. For the tools, we can think together about:

- How are the tools used and by whom? How can students help design, adapt, and use tools?
- What happens to the tools and the ideas embedded in them over time?

Remember that the tools are supposed to help scaffold student thinking and to publicly represent their thinking over time. Finally, I encourage you to create and share repositories of the tools you design. As we create tools to help students, teachers, and administrators disrupt epistemic injustice and create powerful science communities, we need to learn with and from each other's wisdom and work. I cannot wait to see what tools you design; please share any ideas with me and others.

Part 3: Next Steps

Finally, after thinking about the tasks and tools we want to use to enact equitable science and pedagogical opportunities with students, we need to plan some concrete steps to reimagine our communities. In part 3, we reflect on our evolving thinking and commit to actions we will take in the upcoming days, weeks, and years to shift opportunities for student talk and participation. Let's consider:

- What insights into science practices, teaching practices, and the codevelopment of science communities are you considering after your conversations? What are some new ideas that you are considering now? What sparked these ideas for you?
- How will you use your insights into science practices, teaching practices, and the codevelopment of science communities to make some choices about teaching next week? What will you do during the upcoming week in response to something you learned about science practices, teaching practices, and the codevelopment of science communities?
- How might you collect some data about science practices, teaching practices, and the codevelopment of science communities given your plan?

SIX

Tensions, Complexities, and Learning to See Opportunities

THE FIRST FIVE CHAPTERS have been about disrupting epistemic injustice, creating powerful and equitable classroom communities, and considering our roles as teachers and administrators in the design of learning opportunities for students. In addition, I hope we created and used networks of colleagues to help our collective thinking, planning, and enactment of new learning opportunities for students. We have also considered what type of data we should collect to illustrate student learning in powerful classroom communities. I hope that you are considering how to further reimagine your classrooms and schools.

While there is a positive tone and spirit to the book and our collective conversations, we must acknowledge and consider the complexities that are inherent in the work of reimagining classrooms and schools. Recognizing that tensions and complexities exist is important because we can name challenges we face and can think together about how to overcome such obstacles. In addition, considering and conversing about tensions and challenges acknowledges that our classrooms and schools are real places with real students, parents, and other people shaping how our work unfolds. Trying to disrupt injustices that are historically embedded can be difficult, and naming our challenges helps us to move forward together.

In this chapter, we will consider the tensions and complexities of our work in two ways. First, we will revisit Anna's classroom to see how she identified and attempted to navigate complexities. After Anna's example, we will think broadly about other tensions that might arise, and how we might collectively move forward to reimagine classroom communities.

EXAMPLE FROM ANNA

When I participated in Anna's classroom for a two-week unit during the middle of the school year, I was amazed as she used students' science ideas as a foundation for her daily instructional practice. Since the beginning of the year, Anna worked to shift the classroom culture to become a place in which students felt safe to share science ideas. During this unit about energy transformations in roller coasters, students readily discussed their science ideas and, in turn, shaped Anna's daily instructional decisions.

To begin the unit, Anna and her students discussed how they wanted to study potential and kinetic energy, building on previous units. This conversation illustrates the first complexity for Anna—how to use students' ideas to shape the science under investigation. The students noted that a roller coaster seemed similar to skateboarding down a hill, which was the phenomenon of the previous unit. While Anna suggested that the class learn about a new phenomenon, the majority of students wanted to expand the previous unit's phenomenon. Using a class vote, Anna and the students decided to focus on roller coasters. For homework, Anna asked her students to find a video of a crazy roller coaster that they wanted to investigate.

The next day, several students showed videos of roller coasters, and the class voted to investigate a roller coaster going through a loop twice—once forward and again backward. For Anna, here was another moment of complexity: she understood principles of potential and kinetic energy but had not yet constructed her own explanation for the roller coaster.

Next, students watched a video of the roller coaster, recording observations of where they thought energy existed in the roller coaster and how energy transformations might occur. Anna also asked the students to create hypotheses about why the roller coaster could go through the loop twice.

After recording observations and hypotheses, Anna and her students moved to the idea space, a physical location at the back of the room in which students shared their own science ideas as Anna inscribed them on poster paper. By utilizing the idea space, Anna provided opportunities for students to share science ideas in a safe environment. In turn, Anna gave herself opportunities to hear students' thinking that she would not have access to if she shut down their public theorizing. Anna described what she was listening for during this time in the idea space:

> I was listening mostly for talk about height being an indicator of energy and movement being an indicator of energy. I was also listening for talk about other types of energy that exist here, heat from friction, sound, etc. I was also listening for any talk about how potential energy, height energy, gravity energy, turns into kinetic energy, motion energy, moving energy, speed energy. Now that I know what my students are thinking, I know what to do tomorrow.

In other words, Anna wanted to hear and record how students talked about relationships between energy types in order to know what pedagogical decisions to make for the next class period.

The next day, Anna enacted a task that her department mandated be part of the unit: identifying relationships between energy and the height of ramps using wooden blocks. Here, Anna faced another tension. Anna noted that the "external forces" (her department) drove some instructional decisions: "I have to do the lab and return the materials the next day." However, Anna did not waiver from her work to create an equitable classroom community, declaring that her department "could not decide how my students should talk about ideas and evidence in a collaborative way."

As the wooden-block activity progressed, Anna developed questions to ask students in the spur of the moment because:

> It occurred to me during first and second periods that kids weren't able to explain the difference between "the gravity" in the low ramp versus high ramp. I wanted to point out the directional components without overwhelming them to get at kids who need a challenge. For

kids who don't need that complex of a challenge, having them try to articulate working *more* against gravity or *more directly* against gravity was a way to get them to think about the other forces involved. Thinking about gravity overcoming the friction of the block helps reinforce thinking about *net force* instead of just gravity. [observation debrief; italics indicate Anna's emphasis on the words]

Note that Anna reflected on her students' ideas from one class to quickly make a pedagogical decision; she realized she needed to ask different kinds of questions to point out particular aspects of the block-and-ramp phenomenon. This is a great example of Anna using students' science ideas in an earlier class period to make an instructional decision, thus opening up learning opportunities that she did not have in earlier periods.

After the roller coaster video and wooden-block activity, Anna decided to create an explanatory model on a poster during a whole class discussion. Anna used another tool—a red light/green light poster—to scaffold students' participation in the whole class model.* Using this tool, students refuted or added strength to hypotheses and claims using evidence. Anna decided to try the tool because "I wanted an ongoing visual of what we have explained, what we have questions about ... It also 'forces' students to come to a consensus using data and evidence and then discuss their ideas as a class." Note that Anna chose not to employ school-based tools to help students use evidence; rather, she used a tool from a friend and colleague because she understood how it fit into her efforts to reimagine the classroom community.

Using the red light/green light board, Anna and her students used evidence from the wooden-block activity to discuss how the roller coaster traveled through the same loop twice. After a whole class discussion, Anna drew the initial roller coaster model and placed it at the front of the room, thinking that her act of drawing might save time and help move conversations along faster.

For the next class, Anna decided that students should recreate the model she drew. By allowing students to use materials to make a physical model with pipe insulation and a marble acting as the car, Anna gave students opportunities to

---

* This is the same tool that Lindsay used in her ivy unit and that is described in chapter 1. Anna and Lindsay learned about this tool from another teacher colleague who invented the tool to consider evidence about competing hypotheses.

share science ideas while working together to test the whole class model. Subsequently, Anna heard science ideas from students who rarely spoke in class, a good indication that students enjoyed the emerging classroom community.

One critical conversation for the classroom community—and especially for Anna and the students to disrupt epistemic injustice—occurred between two students, José and Anthony, who rarely spoke in class. While attempting to recreate Anna's roller coaster model using copper pipe tubing and a marble (to represent the car), José and Anthony noticed that the marble kept "flying off of the tracks" and that they "can't make it stay on." When they summoned Anna to their table and she observed several trials, she and the boys concluded that José and Anthony's data problematized Anna's model, and that her drawing was incorrectly representing the actual roller coaster.

Anna decided in the moment to recast her unit by leveraging the students' evidence and asked José and Anthony to share their results with the class. After José and Anthony shared their findings, Anna told the class, "Well, there goes my model. Even though you think teachers are always right, this time, your data prove otherwise." When I asked Anna why she allowed José and Anthony to publicly disprove her model, she replied, "Correcting the class model is a good way to give credence to their [students'] ideas ... I want to go where they want to go." Note that Anna both recast her plan, given José and Anthony's evidence, and set herself up as someone who needed to learn from students' science ideas during the remainder of the unit.

Since Anna's model acted as the sole representation of a roller coaster thus far, the class now faced a scientific challenge, and as a teacher, Anna faced another pedagogical decision. Anna asked students to generate a better model since her representation no longer held up against the evidence students compiled in class. Eventually, the students determined that the problem with Anna's roller coaster model was that the car started too high up on a ramp; therefore, the car had too much kinetic energy to remain on the track. The students demonstrated this phenomenon by contrasting how a marble rolling down pipe tubing would always fall off the tubing when constructed to look like Anna's model but would always roll down the tubing successfully if the angle of the initial ramp was lowered (the initial observation made by José and Anthony). The students lowered the height of the ramp, thus reducing the kinetic energy of the car, and successfully revised both the physical and conceptual model.

Generating and testing these new models required two extra days of work that took Anna off the suggested curriculum pace. She decided to give students the opportunity to construct a better model because "lots of students who rarely talk are leading groups, like José and Anthony. I want them to feel empowered to be scientists"—a purposeful stance to disrupt epistemic injustice in her classroom.

After the unit ended, Anna reflected on her teaching and the emerging classroom community, noting that she began the unit planning to teach about types of energy as identified in the district curriculum. However, she realized that her initial planning was limited with respect to students' intellectual capabilities and the classroom community's norms of participation:

> Kids already had a bunch of science ideas about this content, such as forces, velocity, and acceleration—my focus has become teaching them to articulate science ideas both by using the language and by putting the pieces together into an understandable explanation. I've just gotten a much better understanding of the big picture in terms of how energy and forces are related—so my ideas about how to teach this next time is much more clear. It's changed because as I've taught, I've had to think about different pieces of it—so my thinking has changed as a result of me doing more research and asking more questions as well as kids asking questions to make me think about things in a different way.

Note that Anna's recognition and use of students' ideas, and her willingness to make teaching decisions that might deviate from school expectations, opened up opportunities for students that might otherwise have been unavailable. However, Anna navigated complex pedagogical decisions during planning, teaching, and reflection that were difficult.

ZOOMING OUT: NAVIGATING TENSIONS AND COMPLEXITIES

As teachers and administrators, we need to consider our dual roles as adults positioned by society as authorities with scientific and pedagogical expertise yet representing the important feature of equitable classrooms in which we constantly learn, ask questions, and admit the limits of our knowledge. Central to this dual positioning is for us to consider how and when to serve each role. For example, at times, we must use students' knowledge and experiences to help advance the classroom work. We might purposefully inject content into conversations and activities so that students and the classroom community can advance their collective thinking. During other times, we might not know how to move forward and can work with students to consider the ideas, actions, and knowledge needed to move forward as a class.

To consider how we can navigate our role as a teacher and administrator, we need to consider three complexities that will arise in our schools and classrooms.

Is Science Helpful or Harmful?

In chapter 2, as teachers and administrators, we thought about our need to confront what we think counts as science and consider how students should contribute to the scientific knowledge of classrooms. In addition, we must disrupt the notion that science is linear, conducted by genius individuals (usually White men), and objective. However, there is another crucial tension about science in classrooms to confront. First, the version of science that is always beneficial for society does not align with how many people—especially marginalized people—experience the processes and outcomes of science. Given examples in the United States such as Henrietta Lacks and the involuntary extraction of her cells, the Tuskegee syphilis horrors inflicted on Black people, and Monsanto's disproportionate impacts on Black and Brown farmers, we should never pretend that science is neutral in terms of race, class, and politics.[1] As teachers and administrators, we must decide how to help students see the benefits and tragedies of science and consider how to support students in becoming change agents of scientific disciplines.

Whose Ideas Matter?

A second important complexity to navigate, especially as we work together to consider reimagining our classrooms, is that we might think about power, participation, teaching, and learning differently from each other. Consider all the examples of Lindsay's and Anna's classrooms in this book and think about whether you agree, disagree, or wonder about their instructional decisions.

Likely, if we were placed in the same moment and position as Lindsay and Anna, we might say different words and take different actions. As we work together, we need to recognize that as people with power, we are not a monolithic group and therefore have different interpretations of knowledge, practices, and powerful classroom communities. While some of us might try to recognize and elevate certain ideas and experiences from students, others might dismiss such ideas and experiences (and vice versa). Such tensions lead to questions that as teachers and administrators, we must confront: How should ideas from marginalized knowers shape our schools and classrooms? Should all ways of knowing be included, or should criteria be developed to decide which ideas should be considered? How might we transform our classrooms and schools to support knowledge from marginalized people?

Do We Perpetuate Injustice?

A third complexity to consider is that as teachers and administrators, we must think deeply about to whom do we owe an "education debt," given how schooling and science have been used historically to harm and marginalize the communities of many students (especially Black and Brown students).[2] A complex aspect of this conversation is thinking about communities that believe that they are currently harmed by classrooms and schools, but are actually part of dominant groups, and are working to perpetuate epistemic injustice under auspices of marginalization.[3] Therefore, as teachers and administrators, we must ask: What is marginalized, in what ways, and in relation to whom? How do we ensure that the voices of the most impacted are elevated rather than those who claim oppression in order to perpetuate injustice?

As we continue to think together as teachers and administrators, we must remember that classrooms and schools have the potential to set new conditions that promote knowledge diversity and to negotiate new means of knowledge production. However, as philosopher and colleague Kristie Dotson reminds us, "[T]o communicate, we all need an audience willing and capable of hearing us."[4] Thus, the onus is on us, as teachers and administrators, to listen, learn, and actively disrupt epistemic injustice that can harm children. Despite all the potential tensions and challenges we face, we must remember that our goal is to help all students feel safe and valued in our spaces of science learning.

CONCLUDING EXERCISES

Let's engage in two exercises that will help us think about how we can grapple with and navigate potential tensions and complexities around science, teaching, and developing powerful classroom communities. As with every round of exercises, we learn with and from each other as colleagues, so I encourage everyone to create groups to help each other think out loud about the questions.

Exercise 1: How can we recognize and work through pedagogical complexities?

One of the most important roles we have as teachers and administrators is to provide students with opportunities to see and participate in the complexities and messiness of science knowledge practices. Therefore, we need to think deeply about how we represent what counts as science, even the complexities. We also need to account for our talk and actions as teachers as we decide—often in the moment—how to treat students' ideas. Exercise 1 includes questions to consider as we think about the complexities of reimagining our classroom communities.

- When a student says something I do not expect, what is my first thought? Why did I have that specific thought?
- When should I inject content into conversations?
- How should I respond when students ask a question or say something that I do not understand?
- How can I work with students to name questions and problems that we do not know, and consider how to answer or solve such questions and problems?
- What are some specific talk moves I can make, and actions that I can take, to (a) show students how my knowledge and experiences are useful, and (b) negotiate the norms and actions through which students and I will admit the limits of our understanding and signal how we can learn with and from each other?
- At the larger system level, how can schools make building- or district-wide initiatives to take these steps into further action?
- What tensions or challenges exist? How can I navigate them?

- How can we show students that science is open and ongoing rather than linear and terminal after one investigation?
- How can we use or create tools to help students engage in complex science in classrooms (such as leaving lingering questions and incomplete explanations for another class period).
- How can we use classroom science to identify and solve local or community problems?

Exercise 2: What I do need to be successful?

Given the complexities we are discussing, let's think together about what we need to engage in this work with students in our classrooms and schools. As Anna and Lindsay illustrate in their classrooms, disrupting epistemic injustice and reimagining classroom communities require that we ask hard questions of ourselves and our schools. Since teaching is such a personal endeavor—we pour ourselves into this work because we care so much about children—we also need to feel safe and supported to examine our teaching, classroom communities, and opportunities for students. Therefore, we need to think together about the types of support we need to take initial and ongoing steps to reimagine our classroom communities. Here are some sentence starters and questions that can help us begin to reflect and talk with each other about our hopes, worries, and goals for students and classrooms:

- What is exciting about reimagining my classroom and school? Why?
- What worries do I have about reimagining my classroom and school? Why?
- To start taking concrete actions in my classroom, what do I need? Who can help provide support for these needs?
- What support do I need from administrators and colleagues to reimagine my classroom community?
- What difficult questions might administrators, colleagues, and community members (such as parents) ask about my efforts? What conceptual answers about *why* this work is important, and concrete answers about the daily practices, talk moves, and evidence of learning, can I provide about my work?

- How can I ask for help as my work moves forward?
- What will success look like over time? In a week? A month? A year?
- How do I celebrate the joys of the journey with students, colleagues, and administrators?

SEVEN

Shared Goals for Schools and Communities

AS WE HAVE SEEN in Anna's and Lindsay's classrooms, the moment-to-moment interactions between teachers and students, as well as efforts to create equitable classroom communities, can result in powerful opportunities for students. In addition, Anna and Lindsay gave themselves opportunities to grow as teachers. We have also considered the role of administrators in supporting teachers such as Anna and Lindsay to reimagine their classrooms. Now, we need to think about our collective efforts to disrupt epistemic injustice in schools.

As you may have experienced, teachers and administrators do not always make time to discuss shared goals, to understand each other's perspectives, and to think together about creating powerful sites of learning in schools. Yet, we know that teachers and administrators need each other. To achieve powerful and equitable sites of learning, teachers and administrators can work together to have a shared vision, goals, and efforts to support students.

In this chapter, we will consider how teachers and administrators can work together to disrupt epistemic injustice and to reimagine schools as places of learning. We will begin with examples from Anna and Lindsay in which both teachers partnered with administrators to work toward shared goals. We then consider how our work together can help accomplish complex goals. Finally, we will think about how to advocate for change with outside colleagues—such as researchers and policy makers—to collectively reimagine their roles in schools.

WORKING TOWARD SHARED GOALS

Teachers and administrators play a crucial role in setting the vision of classrooms and schools. When they work together to establish a shared vision for places of learning, the feeling of coherence and excitement is powerful. Sadly, however, we are also likely to have experienced a school where there was no shared vision of equity, words, and actions. When teachers and administrators do not share a vision and, worse, are opposed to each other, the challenges and tensions ripple across the school and into students' experiences. In this section, we'll look at examples from Anna and Lindsay in which they worked with administrators toward shared goals for their students. Their attempts at creating shared goals and taking collective action toward the goals show how teachers and administrators can create mutually beneficial partnerships that enable a collective effort to reimagine classrooms and schools.

In Anna's school, there were many multilingual and translingual students. District administrators, who were aware of their community's linguistic needs, began conversations with schools about supports that teachers and principals could design for students. One interpretation of the district's request was that multilingual and translingual students needed opportunities to engage in disciplinary writing, such as using historical documents to make a claim about current politics and creating mathematical proofs using ideas from logic. Of course, students were also expected to engage in scientific writing. Since Anna's district used the NGSS as a guide, district leaders hoped that students might use evidence to make claims, construct explanations for phenomena, and engage in argumentation.

Anna's school decided to emphasize students' written explanation of phenomena as a major goal for the school year. However, given all the constraints schools face, the science teaching team did not have time or space to collaboratively plan how to support students' writing. Therefore, each teacher was left to determine how they might facilitate students' writing without schoolwide goals or support.

Given the school's charge, Anna created a series of scaffolds for students' participation in various forms of scientific writing. Over the next few months, as students and Anna began to trust each other and form a classroom community, the students felt safe to share more and more of their ideas in writing. Sometimes, they would write multiple pages to explain phenomena, and everyone in the class began to feel pride that they could express their thinking to each other. Toward December of the school year, Anna was so proud of her students that she asked her classes if she could display their writing in the hallway outside the classroom. Anna wanted to showcase every student in the class on the wall and worked out a system with the students to ensure that everyone's ideas could have a place for the school to view.

One week after Anna began displaying the students' writing samples on the hallway wall outside her classroom, the principal walked down the science wing of the school, peeking into classrooms. According to the principal, she walked past Anna's classroom, glanced at the wall, walked past, and then backed up to stare at the students' work. The principal had three immediate thoughts: (1) students are writing such long and rich explanations of science phenomena, (2) Anna must be doing something stellar to facilitate students' writing, (3) we, as a school, need to learn from Anna's teaching to help all students—regardless of subject matter—record their thinking in similar writing. Subsequently, the principal positioned Anna as a leader and facilitator of meetings between teacher-colleagues in which they co-constructed scaffolds for student writing and considered how to reframe their classroom communities so that students would feel safe to share their ideas.

As the principal and Anna realized they had overlapping goals for students, they worked together to create opportunities for other students on a schoolwide scale. Importantly, the collective effort to support students' writing through scaffolds was not a top-down mandate that the principal declared necessary for every teacher. Instead, people in the school, already facing a vague set of objectives from district administrators, decided to collectively learn from each other's efforts, to consider evidence of student learning (and writing) across disciplines, and to take initiative to name student success rather than wait for further instructions from people who were absent from the daily life of the school.

Lindsay also encountered similar mandates from her school and district to improve students' outcomes (which, as we know, if often is code for "standardized test scores") without guidance or support from administrators. Like Anna, Lindsay embarked on multiple efforts to create new opportunities for her students, and she invited administrators to be part of the work. For example, given the NGSS push for students to engage in science practices, Lindsay frequently asked her students to name phenomena and problems about the natural world that they wanted to investigate. Rather than shut down those wonderments and dreams, Lindsay reached out to local scientists at cancer centers, health and fitness initiatives, biomedical research facilities, and a large public university to provide insights, ideas, data, equipment, and support for her students.

As she was actively building partnerships with community organizations, Lindsay openly invited school administrators into her classroom to see how the students negotiated and enacted the science work. In addition, Lindsay wanted the administrators to see evidence of student learning and participation that extended beyond the standardized test scores the district valued. Rather than have administrators sit at the back of the room and record private notes, Lindsay encouraged them to participate in the science work alongside students, helping to construct explanations for phenomena, revise models, and weigh evidence to support or refute hypotheses. By encouraging administrators to participate with students in the classroom work, Lindsay helped them see how her instruction shaped students' talk and actions. Such participation also showcased how classroom communities could become places where students created science with teachers, which prompted the administrators to support Lindsay's colleagues in shifting their classroom communities.

Anna's and Lindsay's classrooms provide at least three lessons that stand out in their work. First, Anna and Lindsay used artifacts of student work as evidence of learning in their powerful classroom communities. Rather than rely on rhetoric, Anna and Lindsay showcased students' ideas and learning as outcomes of the classroom communities, thus illustrating that their efforts to reimagine classrooms resulted in profound shifts in student participation. Second, Anna and Lindsay advocated for students and their classroom communities by inviting administrators into classrooms to see what science can look like and to become active community participants. By helping administrators feel welcome in their classrooms, Anna and Lindsay opened doors to communication and action. Third, Anna and Lindsay worked with administrators to identify areas of shared interest in supporting students. By working to name shared interests and goals, the teachers and administrators could find places of agreement to begin supporting students in science classrooms and across the school.

THINKING CONCEPTUALLY

Anna and Lindsay's classrooms provide useful examples of how we—as teachers and administrators—can partner around shared goals. Let's also look at this collective work from a conceptual perspective so that we can consider how we might frame similar opportunities in our classrooms and schools.

When we think about reimagining our communities, our assumptions about authority and power often cause us to perpetuate epistemic injustice. Since we are teachers and administrators, we assume that our job is to know everything and to control students' minds and bodies. In turn, students are supposed to serve as "technicians"; they observe someone else's disciplinary practices and mimic the work deemed important by scientists, science educators, and various materials (such as standard and curricula), but do not have opportunities to shape the knowledge production in classrooms.[1]

We must question our assumption about control over science, ideas, and minds as we design opportunities for students to help shape the work of classrooms and schools. As colleagues, we need to think together about our individual and collective assumptions and to work together to codesign new opportunities with students. Let's also emphasize the term *codesign*: teachers, administrators, and students should negotiate new forms of work, rules, and solutions to problems, often in real time.[2] Such work might initially seem difficult because we might assume that every person, by simply existing in a location, is treated on equal terms as every other person. We must remember to account for inherent power differences between adults and children. Therefore, we need to consider how, as adults with power, we might purposefully help elevate students to the same plane of activity to codesign science communities and practices with us.

Codesigning Classrooms and Schools

Thinking together as teachers, administrators, and students means that we are engaged in codesign work. By codesign work, I mean that we can simultaneously engineer opportunities and collaborative communities while engaged in a systematic study of how people are participating and learning in our schools.[3] Codesign hinges on all participants having a voice in the design and analysis of opportunities and communities, such as:

- Services that various participants inform and perform
- Established processes by which people can exchange information and ideas
- Ongoing and codeveloped customization of products and practices over time
- Mutual learning from interactions among the community's participants[4]

Thus, in the work of codesign, each participant plays a crucial role in identifying problems, developing solutions, and negotiating practices in order to continue to reimagine and improve classrooms and schools. Community learning occurs as participants confront tensions and reassess the effectiveness of their efforts to solve problems.

Principles for Codesign

Given the importance of codesign, there are three guiding principles that we should consider when initiating and continuing codesign work.

1. *Collective rather than individual work.* As researchers note, for systems—such as classrooms and schools—to shift from historic inequities to new forms of activity, actions must be collective and negotiated among participants rather than privileged among a select few. As we have seen with Anna and Lindsay, reimagining their classrooms and making an impact on student learning in their schools required multiple people—with different forms of power—to negotiate participatory practices and to create shared goals. None of the pedagogical or organizational decisions were the sole responsibility of one person. In other words, no person operated in isolation; rather, many people in a school collectively developed, tested, and revised the norms for participation.

2. *Designing for participation.* As we are learning, people with power (such as teachers and administrators) can design opportunities for students to move from the margins of science to actively shaping classroom and school communities. As we have seen with examples from Anna, Lindsay, and their schools, such opportunities must be purposeful; there should be a shared vision about what counts as science and who is a scientist. The shared vision is important because people do not learn merely content or practices in a setting. Embedded in knowledge and actions are messages about who a person should be—their identity, values, and vision of success.[5] Therefore, there should be coherence across goals for teachers and administrators and a shared understanding of how to act in moments when students offer ideas and interests that could transform participatory norms if recognized and valued.

3. *Navigating uncertainty.* A recurring theme of this book—and the work of reimagining classrooms and schools—is learning to navigate the inherent uncertainty of codesigning science with students. As we have seen, there is often incoherence between the image of science presented by schools (science as a linear and logical progression of experimentally proven facts) and the work of science in the real world (science as meaning-making, given a host of unpredictable factors).[6] As teachers and administrators, we need to recognize and uphold the stance that science, and teaching, must be continually adapted based on emerging (and sometimes unforeseen) needs. We must support each other as we adapt to real-time tensions and surprises, both of which can be destabilizing in positive ways.

As the three principles indicate, codesign hinges on all participants making an active and continuous contribution to the science practices in a classroom and community.[7] Codesign inherently requires everyone—including those who are typically marginalized by people with power—to participate differently in a school that is aiming to disrupt epistemic injustice. For people with power, such as teachers and administrators, we must alter our participation by redistribute some of pedagogical and scientific responsibilities to students. We must also question entrenched rules, norms, and participatory structures so that we can work with students in real time to identify problems and develop solutions—the core of codesign.

BUILDING CONTEXTS OF SUPPORT

Most of this book focuses on the actions of teachers and administrators in a school or classroom to disrupt epistemic injustice and build equitable science communities with students. However, schools and classrooms do not exist in a vacuum; they are part of local communities and larger contexts of education policy and actions. Whether or not we like it, the thoughts and actions of people outside our immediate schools and communities have a direct impact on the decisions (both moment-to-moment and long-term planning) we make about students' learning opportunities. Our work to codesign places of learning should include conversations with stakeholders who exist outside schools, such as community members, policy makers, and researchers. Therefore, let's think together about why such stakeholders might be important for our work, and consider how they might aid in our collective to reimagine classrooms and schools.

Policy Makers

As teachers and administrators, we know that policy makers—whether local, state, or national—can have a huge impact on the day-to-day reality of classrooms and schools. Even if they have not been physically present in a classroom in decades, policy makers' memories, mythologies, and mandates about schools shape decisions made by various stakeholders. In particular, there is a long history of debates between policy makers and teachers about the best learning opportunities needed to support all students in schools.

To facilitate the work of disrupting epistemic injustice and reimagining classrooms, policy makers need to recognize the imbalance of power between the people making laws and recommendations about teaching and the people who actually make day-to-day instructional decisions in classrooms. Rather than preach to teachers about work they have never experienced or understood, policy makers should honor teachers and support their efforts to disrupt epistemic injustice.

Policy makers also have an opportunity to change the course of science teacher education by supporting efforts to recruit and retain great teachers. We need a reimagined system of support and retention in which the definition of teacher and student success that emerged during the No Child Left Behind

Era—the increase in standardized test scores—is finally discarded after a generation of research demonstrates that such testing does not measure the quality of teaching or student learning. Therefore, policy makers can work with partners in schools and teacher preparation programs to identify and evaluate new evidence of success for teachers. In addition, policy makers could take a stance about the professionalization of teaching by rewarding schools and teacher education programs for disrupting assumptions and building equitable and ambitious forms of teaching. Rather than pretend that teachers can learn complex professional work online, policy makers can reward schools and science teacher education programs that make strong community connections and provide opportunities for rehearsals of equitable teaching practices.

Professional Scientists

One way that adults often provide students with a window into professional science (by which I mean science as a career) is to have a local scientist serve as an ambassador in a classroom. For example, you may have experienced initiatives in which scientists make an initial visit to classrooms to talk with students about their research. Following this visit, the scientists return to facilitate an activity or lesson with students. Alternatively, scientists might plan academic field trips in which a teacher works with a scientist to identify a curriculum topic that students will learn. On a prescribed day, the teacher and students travel to the scientist's research site. The scientist then provides space for students to engage in an activity that highlights the curriculum topic.

While each of these examples offers opportunities for scientists, teachers, and students to interact, the scientist appears to be positioned as the sole regulator of knowledge and practices—the solitary person with scientific power. Students remain technicians by observing someone else's disciplinary practices and participate in work the scientist deems important, but do not have opportunities to shape the knowledge production in classrooms.

Therefore, if you are a science professional, you can represent the daily practices, norms, and identity of your field for teachers and students. More importantly, you can partner with schools and classrooms to bring teachers and students into your worksite. When teachers and students are in your sites, let them take on responsibilities beyond cleaning equipment or fetching coffee. Provide opportunities for teachers and students to engage in daily and valued practices of your field, and make public your decision-making and actions. Form long-term partnerships with schools to engage in ongoing research with teachers and students.

Education Researchers

Too often, education researchers—who investigate classrooms and schools—distance themselves from the teachers and administrators. I think of this framing as "doing research on" versus "doing research with" teachers and administrators. Instead of trying to separate themselves from the people engaged in the daily work of reimagining classrooms and schools, I urge education researchers to form partnerships with teachers and administrators so that they can codesign opportunities and investigations that are meaningful to everyone.

Education researchers, then, can play an important role by helping teachers and administrators disrupt their ideas about classrooms and schools and by helping to codesign new sites of learning. Education researchers must uphold the values and actions that they investigate. Education researchers must make their planning, teaching, and decision-making public and open to conversation with teachers and administrators. Such researchers should also represent what they want teaching to look like, including how they create and foster equitable participation structures in classrooms. In sum, education researchers must avoid the hypocrisy of preaching about equitable classrooms and schools, yet not taking concrete actions with teachers and administrators to help create such sites of learning.

As teachers and educators, we know that people with power who make decisions about schools have not always listened to, supported, and encouraged practitioners in schools. Teachers and administrators are often (and purposefully) excluded from conversations among people with power despite the direct impact that such conversations have on classrooms and schools. I argue that while we are responsible for the moment-to-moment interactions that occur in our classrooms, stakeholders outside schools—such as policy makers—need to question the assumptions they hold about teaching and learning. They must listen to, and honor, the voices of teachers and administrators who are working toward reimagining classroom communities and disrupting epistemic injustice.

QUESTIONS TO CONSIDER

As we consider codesign work to disrupt epistemic injustice and to reimagine classroom communities, we should think together about how we might build and foster collaborative partnerships. As a group of teachers and administrators, we could ask questions such as:

1. Who are people in the community with whom we are in regular communication? Whose voices and perspectives are we missing? How might we try to build partnerships with people who are often excluded from our schools?
2. Who are our local, state, and national representatives? How might we invite them to become part of conversations about our needs and changes required in schools? What evidence can we provide them about our successes, and how do we ask for help to overcome challenges?
3. What resources might be available in our communities to engage in powerful and codesigned science work? Are there professional scientists who can partner with the school? Are there opportunities, such as community gardens, to engage in meaningful and local science?
4. What resources and people do we wish we had available to build partnerships? Who could we contact to help acquire, build, or use such resources?

EIGHT

Words of Wisdom from Anna and Lindsay

ANNA AND LINDSAY are still teaching (both in different schools from where the stories from this book emerged) and, as noted, were glad to share their good, challenging, and complex experiences about the work of reimagining classroom communities. I am honored to tell part of their story, but I also want to give Anna and Lindsay the opportunity to speak directly about creating, sustaining, and growing equitable classroom communities. Since their ideas and experiences are providing us with vital examples to guide our conversations, they should have an important voice as we think together. I asked them each six questions about ideas we have discussed in the book, and I lightly edited their answers—all direct quotes—for clarity. I encourage you to use the questions and their ideas as important resources as you begin and continue your work.

QUESTION 1

We know that building relationships and trust with students is one of the top things a teacher needs to do to create equitable and justice-oriented classroom or school communities. We also know that relationships and trust with students is complex work. What are the top things you think about when planning, teaching, and reflecting about creating a classroom community where students feel safe to share ideas and feel like a valued part of the community?

Lindsay and Anna described similar stances and activities about building trust and relationships with students. Lindsay and Anna's responses follow; they are categorized by important ideas that they elevated and described during our conversations.

Purposefully build a safe and collaborative community with students that is adapted over time

LINDSAY: I think there is a lot of fear from teachers thinking that they must stay in a position of power, and if I get down on their level, I'll lose control of the class. But actually, if students feel love and respected, they will want to be in the classroom because it is an important space for them. For example, I had that student who got suspended from school, but she snuck back into school just to come to my science class because she wanted to participate and did not want to let her group down. For most of school, she was characterized as not smart and a troublemaker. But in my class, when she raised her hand to share, it was so exciting. She saw that I cared about her, and that her peers cared about her ideas and experiences. As a teacher, I always validate students so that they feel seen. Everyone wants to feel seen as a human.

One way I begin this process with students is to build agreements with each class about how we want to engage in science work together. There's a big difference between telling students, "Here are my rules for the classroom" and "Let's build the rules and norms together." I also revisit and change community norms with students over time. I think a lot of people start by creating norms with students, but then never come back to the norms, as if the community will participate in the same way for an entire school year. I worry that teachers, and many administrators, go through the motions of building community norms but never really make the codevelopment of a community a really significant part of the class. Maybe they think, "Oh it's a best practice to make a poster with cowritten rules," they put it on the wall, and they never come back to it. Instead, building a community is a process. I often have students write in journals about their strengths and what they are hoping to learn, and then we can think about how our community can help everyone grow. As a teacher, then I can learn a lot about my students by reading their journals. Then on any day, you can revisit norms and student goals and can ask, "How are we doing on these? As a community, how can we help support each other better than we are right now?" I make sure that I am helping my students feel like they have a voice in their learning and in our community's thinking and actions.

ANNA: I want my students to know that we are constantly learning and growing together. I always treat students as constantly learning. If the class is not talking in collaborative ways, then let's figure out together how we can talk to each other. If the class is not following written directions, then let's figure out how we can create directions that they can understand. If students need to know how to talk in a small group, then I need to provide quick, modeled instruction. Even throughout the year, as kids' attention wanes, revisit routines and adapt them. People, but specifically kids, cannot make brave cognitive moves in a space where they do know what to expect or do not feel protected from ridicule. Kids cannot learn science in an authentic way without learning how to make brave cognitive moves.

Create many ways for students to have a voice

LINDSAY: Your words have to match your actions. You cannot say, "There are no stupid questions" and then teach in a way that shuts down questions that you do not like and think are distracting from your agenda. You can say, "That's a good question," but then saying, "But we don't have time to explore that," or "That's off topic," or "I have to get through this lesson," shows that you do not really think the student had a good question. You can say you trust students, but you have to show them that you trust them.

We have such a sense of urgency in teaching—bell to bell! But this is teaching … How can a student learn if they do not feel confident and don't feel like their voice is heard? How can students learn if they don't feel like an intellectual contributor or a valued human in your classroom?

I also want students to bring their interests and passions into the classroom, and I want to learn from their emerging expertise. For example, we did a genetics unit, and we talked about bioethics. Students came to me the next day and week with stories they found online about this unit and similar topics. I should not be ashamed that I've never read these articles or that I did not know about the topics that students read. I should be excited that they are spending time out of class thinking and learning about the issues in their communities. I should be grateful to learn from students and their excitement. Students can and should shape a teacher's thinking because they have an important voice.

ANNA: Some students are comfortable speaking up, and some are not comfortable. For some, it changes by the day (or the hour). Always plan multiple ways into a lesson for students' ideas to get out into the public record. The more chances students have to put their ideas out there, publicly or anonymously, the more likely it becomes that they will take advantage of those opportunities. Over time, they begin to see that you really do want to hear what they have to say. The most shy students will watch as you listen to their classmates, and they will begin to want to engage—and they will find a way that works for them. Examples:

- A written entry task that you walk around and read quickly, over their shoulder. You can ask the student if it's okay for you to share the idea. You can ask them if you may attach their name to it. You can simply say to the whole class, "I saw a great idea in ____'s notebook. Are you willing to share? May I share it for you?"
- A chance to show agreement or disagreement without explaining ("Make some noise if you agree with Rosie's idea, or you said something similar," "Move to the windows if you agree, the door if you disagree, middle if you aren't sure yet").
- A chance to change their minds about something.
- Talk at their tables; then choose one idea to share to the group.
- Anonymous Post-it Note answers to a question.

Whatever gets the students talking and providing evidence from class activities and their lived experiences in communities is helpful.

Be intentional about elevating student ideas

ANNA: Part of my power and responsibility as a teacher is to empower student leaders and to create a community where students want to participate. I actively need to highlight good ideas of students, especially students who do not feel safe to speak, might face personal challenges that make participation difficult, or who may have even been rude to me yesterday. By doing this, I'm showing that I care about student ideas, and that I know every student has good ideas *in their brains, their thinking, and their experiences.*

I also make sure to keep track of who speaks up and who I highlight and praise, and I spread my attention to students over time. Sometimes, the biggest difference for a student can come from taking the time in the moments after class to say, "Hey, Austin, I noticed you spoke up today. Your idea was really helpful to the class, so thanks for pushing yourself today." So much of the time, kids want to feel seen, but they do not necessarily want to feel looked at by everyone. Learning about your students is so crucial, so you know if you should stop class to publicly compliment someone or slip them a written note that they can shred and throw away, keeping their social status as someone who does not care what the teacher thinks—these little intricacies are what communicate to students that you are paying attention to them and know how they tick.

Importantly, another thing that I've learned is to always honor an agreement to keep student anonymity. I often say things like, "Someone had the idea that ____. I'll pause and give the students a moment to claim that idea if they want to." If they choose not to raise their hand or say, "That was mine," I move on and allow them to remain anonymous. Let students take the step of speaking up and sharing when they are ready. They always will, eventually, but it might take *all year.* That's okay, because when they do speak, you can see that you've built a trusting relationship with that students, and hopefully, all students.

Explicitly share your power or "front of the room" space

LINDSAY: As a teacher, I think that I am part of the community, not that I'm the boss of the community. I think and ask students, "What do you need from me? How can I help you?" I'm human, I make mistakes, so I ask students, "What should we do if I make a mistake or cause harm?" And it's not that anyone wants to make mistakes or cause harm (hopefully), but that's part of being human. So we think together about how we can support each other's learning and growing. Teachers being vulnerable and human is very refreshing to students.

ANNA: The classroom does not just belong to you. The classroom must be a space where students see how they have control and where they can effect change. Let students challenge you publicly; take them seriously when they do. For example, if they complain about the bathroom policy ("You're always forgetting who is next!") ask them to come up with a better one; then use it. If a policy is terrible, ask students to change the policy. If you have a kid who hogs airtime, get them in front of the room, facilitating the discussion. If you have a kid who loves to be the center of attention, have them act out the directions that you want the class to follow. Find ways to get your students to run things, then reflect on how it went, and make it better. Students are really just making the classroom a safe place for their learning, and they will take better care of a space where they feel they have a role, a place, a job. Letting students challenge or change the routines in your room (within reason) shows them that you seriously consider them a part of the community, they have a say, and also that they have some responsibility in the group.

See and value students in spaces outside of your classroom and school

LINDSAY: If there is any way to do home visits, do it. A great way to build empathy is to see and learn from students in their homes and places outside of school.

ANNA: You are tired, you are exhausted, you do not think you have time, but stop by the volleyball game anyway and make a point to say hi or wave at your students. Even if your students ignore you, or giggle and whisper to their friend, they saw you. They know you took the time to stop by. Even if it was only five minutes, they'll remember seeing you there. Find something good they did to congratulate them on the next day ("You can serve overhand; impressive!"). Visit other classrooms if you can (and are welcome). Students are not the same person in band as they are in science as they are in fitness. See them as more than just people in your classroom and make clear that you are excited to see them in other places doing cool activities.

Listen to students' parents, guardians, or mentors as they talk about their child. What message is this child receiving at home or in other spaces about their academic potential? I remember one student's father, at conferences, asked how his son was doing in class. I mentioned that he was a leader, using his social capital to share ideas that often pulled the class in the right direction. His dad dismissed the compliment, saying there was no way that I was describing his son—and he was serious. Praising that child (when he earned it) became more urgent after that meeting, to counter the messages he seemed to be getting from home that school was not a place that he was "designed for." Your words have power, and the most important thing you can do for adolescents is *notice them* and let them know that you see who they are trying to be. *And* whatever that is, is wonderful. Even if it changes every day. Let them be who they are and love them for it. This is an important time of their life when they use others' behavior toward them to determine their self-worth; there is really only one message that we should be sending them!

QUESTION 2

To begin building trust, how do you even begin the school year? What are the most important things you can say or do during the first month to build a community with students? How does your role change over time?

LINDSAY: I am always sad that many middle and high school students enter science classrooms already convinced that they are bad at science because of previous experiences in science spaces where adults position them as nonscientists. One of my most important jobs is to help students reimagine what is possible in science classrooms. In the first days, weeks, and month of the school year, I think it is really important to think with students about the purpose of the classroom, the norms for participation, and what counts as success for student learning. Students need to see that we, as teachers, will think with them about how we want the classroom community to grow.

I think to begin the school year, students need to see that we should not rush through building norms just to fast-forward to science. I think many of them have had experiences where the first week is norm-building, and then it is time for the science, as if those features of the class are separate. Doing science and building a community are bound together and take time. If we want students to have engaging and exciting science experiences, then we need to develop a classroom—with students—that allows them to be engaged and excited. Students cannot be engaged and excited in a classroom where they feel scared and feel like they cannot say anything that might be considered "wrong" or "off topic." I also keep repeating to students that learning is different from memorizing information. Learning is actively doing science, building a community, and having a powerful voice in what happens in a classroom.

ANNA: To begin a school year, I think about two main ideas in my role as a teacher. Number one: I think with students about two to three main science routines we will frequently enact together, and we start using those routines from day one. There's no need to overwhelm students; keep things simple so students can get good at a few routines really quickly. As a reference, I usually think about: (1) How do we start class? (2) How do we engage in group talk? (3) How do we share ideas and engage in classroom discussions? Setting a strong start of class routine is super important because it sets the tone for your class. We have signals, such as bell, and such signals help convey when things should occur, such as a do-now or entry task. This routine provides safety because it's the same every single day. It sets the expectation that we start class with thinking and sharing ideas, and it provides a structure so that they know to think about a question individually. We engage in whole classroom conversations soon after (group talk), so we practice talking with our group every single day. This is important because kids need to practice sharing ideas confidently and listening actively to other students. We share out ideas to the whole class and sometimes have a discussion. By the end of the start of class, every student has spoken, and every student has had an idea listened to. While students are doing this, I walk around the room to take attendance and greet every student by name.

Number two, I want time to engage in community and culture building every day for the first month. Even if this time is simply spent by me saying, "Okay, we're going to share what we wrote with our table group. The person who's going to share first is the oldest person at your table," I want students thinking about and engaging in routines to help or the classroom to be a safe place to share ideas. I also want students learning more about each other and finding common ground so that they see each other as great people rather than random people who happen to be in the same space.

QUESTION 3

Some teachers and administrators worry about off-track ideas. What do you say to students, parents, and administrators about student thinking and its importance in the classroom?

LINDSAY: I want anyone who thinks about classrooms—parents, administrators, policy makers—to know that classrooms are supposed to be a place where all questions are valid. Too often, students say, "This is a stupid question, but . . ." or think, "This is a stupid question," so they never ask. In whatever community you are creating with students, the beginning should encourage questions and help students feel like they should wonder about big and complex ideas. Then, move from questioning to sharing ideas. I think it is important to have students feel comfortable to ask questions because sharing ideas feels more vulnerable. As a teacher, you have to validate student questions and thinking. I do not care if the idea is from left field or another galaxy. I need validate the student's thinking and participation. One easy way to validate student thinking is to write their idea on some classroom tool—the whiteboard, a shared Google Document, a poster for the classroom walls.

ANNA: I take the stance that no idea is off-track. Sure, some ideas might be more helpful than others, but I want students to use evidence to revise ideas, not just me tell facts that anyone can look up in a book. I actively record students' initial ideas in a public way (model, list of hypotheses, etc.), and revisit these ideas over time as they gain more evidence. Eventually, the off-track ideas will be eliminated from the public record (and if they are not, you have to maybe add a lesson that will lead to their elimination). If students in your class are actively learning how to use evidence to support or refute ideas (and they should be), this will become a natural routine in your class. But there is value in the off-track ideas, and that's important to share, too. Without off-track ideas, we wouldn't have built science knowledge that the earth is round, that the crust of the earth is broken into pieces that are moving, that giant ice age floods can make ripples in the earth so big that they are rolling hills to us. We need off-track ideas in science in order to make progress. So, even if your idea turns out to be refuted by evidence, it's still useful to the group. Conveying that to kids is simple; just let them pose ideas and give them all a chance to be tested. Take them seriously, and let kids try to prove each other's ideas right or wrong. This is going to increase student engagement in your class, so your administrators are going to love this community.

QUESTION 4

We know that people outside of our classroom have a big influence on what happens in schools. For different groups of people, what do you want them to know about your work as a teacher? How can they help you? What resources or help could you use from them to grow your classroom community?

LINDSAY: I always remind adults that schools and information have changed since we were kids. Teaching is not about delivering information anymore. There is plenty of information online, and amazing people are creating a vast array of simulations, animations, and ways to teach content. Our job as teachers has to shift since the world has changed.

This makes me wonder about the purpose of education and schools. Is the purpose to collect information in your brain or prepare you to be a participant of the world? Is it to discover your passion and talent and share it with the world? I firmly believe that the purpose of education is not to fill students' heads with facts. How is that useful? If the purpose is to get a job, having a bunch of facts in your brain is not going to get you a job. Critical thinking, communication, and teamwork—those are important skills. Where do we learn those? Well, we can learn those in classrooms. Even if you look at how people work now, that's not what schools emphasize.

For example, I do not care about tests, especially standardized tests. If you give a test, let students have all of their notes. What an inauthentic way to know if students are learning by giving them a series of decontextualized questions with one correct answer. When in the adult world will you have to take a blind test without access to the internet or other resources? Learning comes from synthesizing information and doing things. Even if you have to give tests, at least make them like the real world. Give kids a real-world problem, give them access to resources, give them a deadline. You know, like in real life. Or let them work in a group. How many jobs are completely isolated and you never interact with anyone else?

Then maybe people might ask, "How do we know kids are learning?" Easy! Performance tasks. Here's a rich problem to solve—a challenge that people are actually working on, and maybe the kids have good ideas about how to solve the challenge that they can share with adults. A design process. You need knowledge for this, but it is knowledge with a purpose. We underestimate what kids are capable of and how much they can help shape the knowledge of the world. They can go such much deeper than we give them credit for in classrooms and schools. Sure, this work requires scaffolding, but kids are way smarter and can think about complex issues, and we need administrators and policy makers to trust teachers to really help kids succeed.

ANNA: There are two main things I wish people outside classrooms would help teachers with so that we can help students learn. First, people always talk about teacher pay. We must create conditions—including good pay—that help recognize teachers as professionals. Things like sick leave and mental health leave are also crucial, as society has started to blame teachers for everything wrong in the world. Trust us, pay us, and let us help your kids learn.

Second, standardized testing is poorly executed and is a terrible indicator of student learning and of my teaching. Even if the tests were good (which they are not yet, and maybe never will be), the data come to teachers too late to be useful for kids. The data are super useful for labeling schools as failing, but the data should be *useful to kids*! That means, as a teacher—if my students take a test in grade 8, I'd like that info to be available to their grade 9 science teacher. Logistically, these things are so poorly communicated, and also data are locked down so only a test administrator can often see it—so teachers do not get that information. Test scores are also often just not super accurate. I do not give typical exams in my class (like true or false and multiple choice), so how would a traditional exam measure my students' progress? Students are writing arguments and creating physical models and learning to talk to each other. How can a test measure that learning?

QUESTION 5

How might a teacher start reimagining their classroom community from a lens of equity and justice?

LINDSAY: Middle and high school teachers—especially general science teachers—feel this impostor syndrome, that they always have to be correct and be in charge: "I cannot be a teacher if I do not know everything." Thinking you are supposed to be the ultimate content and instructional authority is not the place to be if you want to be a good teacher. You cannot be open, vulnerable, and human with your students if you think you are supposed to know everything and be a science robot. I think as a teacher, there is a fear of being found out that I do not know everything. No one can know everything, and new discoveries about what we have already taught happen all of the time. Things I taught about in my first year of teaching are already being refined as we learn more about them. My advice is to let go of the fear and worry about being the teaching and content boss. It is exhausting to think that I should always be the boss of children.

If you are teaching in a lecture-information-delivery way, then there is too much pressure on you to be the authority and holder of all content. That is too much pressure and exhaustion. Rather than feeling like "I have to be the expert on my domain," I think we should be the facilitators of learning and be great designers of learning opportunities that empower students to become advocates for their learning to develop confidence. I know that it may feel scary to let kids have a strong voice in shaping the classroom community, but this also makes teaching much more fun and enjoyable.

Beyond you on a personal level, you have to make the classroom a place where students' lives, communities, and experiences intersect around science in a positive way. When you give students opportunities to share, encourage them to draw on their life experiences. They have such rich lives outside of school, and the more you can help them make connections between outside and school, the more they see that their lived experiences are important, that they matter in school, and that they are scientific. I had a student say, "I go skateboarding in the skate park, now I am connecting skating it to Newton's laws of motion, and I know why tricks do not work because of physics." Students can see that everything is connected.

Beyond science, you have to get to know students as people. I do exit tickets as a survey—content and noncontent questions. For example, students can request a song on an exit ticket, and I will play the song as they walk into class; then they know that I care enough to read their ideas and download a song that they like and play it for everyone.

I also help students set goals—academic and personal—and then check with kids about their goals. Especially out-of-school goals—this helps build relationships. Then you can see if a lot of kids like something, like soccer, how can I build that into class? I also start class with journaling—content and noncontent, like if you could start a restaurant, what food would it serve—and so then they share ideas with each other. They get to know each other and get to see that our community has all of these experiences and ideas. Kids want to talk to each other, so we should figure out how to build in opportunities for talk that are also opportunities for community building.

ANNA: I am very thankful to have a community of colleagues who helps me think about creating equitable classrooms. I think teachers should help each other do this work; we are all in this together to help students. My primary way of thinking about a unit or lesson is all about access and letting kids talk. I have three principles:

1. Let kids talk about their ideas.
2. Let kids test their ideas.
3. Present them evidence that either supports or refutes their ideas and ask them to talk about it again.

Remember that kids, and us as teachers and administrators, need to learn and practice how we engage with each other and with ideas. School is for learning, so we need to make sure that our classroom community supports the learning of how we interact and create science.

Super importantly, as teachers we need to know that we have to create a safe place for kids to feel vulnerable. Teenagers are going to protect themselves from looking stupid or wrong until they are convinced that the classroom safe. While there is a time and a place to tell a student that their idea is wrong, in the past ten years of teaching, I find that these times are few and far between, because *other students* can do that job for you—and isn't that more authentic science anyway? It's peer review!

Allowing student ideas to shape the class is a big equity move because it gives value to their voices, *even if they might be wrong.* It gives this idea that everyone has a place. If you feel like it might flop, just tell kids what you're doing and why. ("Okay, we're sharing a ton of ideas today. We might figure out later that some are wrong, but I don't care about that right now! Right now we just need a list. A big list! What ideas might you have if you weren't afraid to be wrong? What ideas might you have if it didn't matter if you were right?") Adults spend so much time telling kids that they are wrong that we forget how brilliant and creative they are, and how their ideas are often so much less limited than ours. I still learn from my students. I love when they challenge me. I let them—I encourage them to, so we can test our ideas and figure it out. That's what science *is!*

For a teacher who is truly tentative, though, I'd say just try it with a simple mini-phenomenon. Show kids something puzzling, ask for their ideas, chart them. Then, give them a lab or investigation that will help them see if they are correct or not, and ask them to go back and revise their original ideas. Start small! Kids will eventually learn to trust that you really want them to build knowledge.

These principles are even more important anytime there are more power dynamics in the room than just teacher-student. If you are a White teacher (like me), it is extra important that you are attentive to how you are responding to your kids of color when they speak up. If you identify as male, the same thing applies. The choices you make as a teacher model for your students how they should behave in the world of science. They model who they should listen to. If you simply always call on the White boy with his hand up, you send a message, whether you like it or not. It doesn't take a lot of effort to find ways to elevate other voices in the room, and the payoff is huge as kids begin to see that everyone's input has value.

QUESTION 6

As teachers, we are never finished learning. What questions do you still have? What challenges do you still encounter?

LINDSAY: I have two main questions. First, I think about the system of education, especially higher education. You go K–12, and then you go to college to get a job. Why is that the way we frame it? Going to college does not guarantee you a job, and you should feel free to explore what you love. Second, education is being reimagined in K–12, but I worry that it is not being reimagined in higher education. If we do all of this amazing work shifting K–12 STEM education but universities don't change, what will students experience? Why would there be this disconnect between what we do in K–12 and what we do in higher education?

ANNA: I continue to struggle with the balance between having control in my classroom and giving control to kids. In those moments when I feel it's appropriate to give control to kids (i.e., let them steer the discussion or investigations), I am almost never disappointed with the creativity and brightness that follows. Yet I continue to place a lot of value on "my time" that I have spent creating and curating an experience for students; it is a lot of work to truly adapt each day and be flexible with students and their ideas.

I also continue to struggle with the system—even in the international school where I now work, we are moving toward a schedule where I will be teaching two, possibly three different courses (multiple sections) over a cycle of two days in addition to an advisory class. While the goal of this is to broaden choices for kids, the net result is (and *always seems to be*) to give more work to teachers. It's as if, even after all this time, no one really understands how much time (and how many brains) it takes to design a unit, *but then also teach it in a responsive way that is constantly collecting real-time data about what kids can do and what they still need to learn to do.* That constant knowledge that people really don't understand what I do—the mental load of it all—is frustrating to me. Teachers carry a lot in their brain. The better you get at it, the more you carry. And I continue to struggle with the negative impacts of that load. Because I really do see magic happen in my classroom, so I know it's good work. But at some point, it's at the expense of the individuals doing the work, and that's why so many people leave. I continue to say, "No, thank you," to leadership positions and extra things so I can really focus on my classroom—and I think that is okay. We have a lot of fun, we learn a lot, and to be honest I'm still learning a lot of science these days (mostly physics and astronomy) from my students. They are so smart, often smarter than me.

As you can see, Lindsay and Anna have both reflected deeply about their classroom communities and the day-to-day work of disrupting epistemic injustice. I hope that their ideas can provide a catalyst for you and your team to begin the work of creating powerful and equitable learning spaces for students.

NINE

Moving Forward

Action Research

I HOPE THAT THIS BOOK and our time together have been useful catalysts for you and your communities to launch important work together. The ideas and exercises of this book can be a useful resource as you continue to reimagine classroom and school communities, and work to actively disrupt epistemic injustice. In the spirit of continued work together, this chapter has two parts to help you begin your work: a few thoughts about how to use this book during professional learning opportunities, and a suggestion to engage in action research to help you begin your important work.

WORKING TOGETHER

Moving forward, you can use the wisdom of Lindsay and Anna—as well as the knowledge you develop together—as launching pads for reimagining classrooms and schools through a lens of disrupting epistemic injustice and promoting equitable learning spaces. Throughout this book, I have suggested that you form a community of learners—teachers, administrators, and other colleagues (as well as community members)—to help begin and advance conversations. Now let's think together about how these conversations might unfold and remember that we are always learning and growing together.

As you begin the conversations, remember that the main goal is to create a safe and trusting community in which people can share ideas, ask questions, work though challenges, and learn with and from each other. In short, we are trying to create a powerful learning community of teachers and administrators that reflects the values and goals for our classrooms and schools. In our learning communities, remember that everyone is approaching the conversation from different perspectives, having different life experiences and holding different assumptions about science and teaching. We need to understand each other's perspectives and work toward developing a shared understanding and goals to reimagine our classrooms and schools.

To create productive conversations, I have four suggestions that I have adapted from a wonderful discussion guide written by colleagues Dr. Tanya Maloney and Dr. Bree Picower.[1] First, the team can decide on a lead organizer or conversation facilitator for each session. Perhaps the same person decides to take on this role or perhaps the role rotates. Either way, having a lead person who can organize and facilitate conversations can help the discussion and actions move toward actionable outcomes.

Second, before each meeting, decide what parts of the book to use and which ideas you want to discuss during a particular conversation. Your team could decide to read the entire book before meeting or could have multiple sessions in which one or a few chapters are discussed. Either way, the team should know the depth of the task, given how busy we all are as teachers and administrators.

Third, remember that everyone enters the conversation at different places and holds varied assumptions about the world. Create norms for talk to allow time for thinking, to celebrate successes, and to constantly consider how we can help each other grow. In addition, we must support each other to unpack assumptions, to define and describe ideas, and to ask hard questions about how to move forward.

Fourth, everyone should be prepared for the conversation and for next steps. Clearly, everyone should do the reading and agree to the structure of the sessions. In addition, everyone should commit to taking future steps that the team decides and must advocate for each other's success as the team is learning together.

ACTION RESEARCH

As you and the team are learning together and planning concrete actions to reimagine classrooms and schools, you can consider engaging in action research. Like Anna and Lindsay, you can begin to collect evidence of student learning; can present the evidence to local, state, and national leaders; and can write about your work in various venues (blog posts, science education journals for teachers; see later). Here are some general suggestions about action research. (If you are interested, there are wonderful resources available to help you start the work, such as the book by Dr. Marilyn Cochran-Smith and Susan Lytle titled Inquiry as Stance: Practitioner research for the next generation.)

The idea of action research is to identify a problem of practice, develop a plan for your classroom and school, implement the plan, and engage in evidence-based reflection on how your plan helped students learn. Action research can certainly be conducted individually, but as I have noted throughout, participating with a team of colleagues who are engaged in similar work can help everyone's efforts to reimagine classrooms and schools.

While there is not a single or linear way to conduct action research, here are some phases of the work that might provide some signposts and guidance as you work together.

Description of the Problem of Practice

There are many ways in which epistemic injustice is perpetuated in classrooms and schools, and many ways to reimagine how we can create and support students to engage in powerful science. One important task to complete at the beginning of the work (and revisit throughout) is to name and describe a situation, problem, or issue that you and your group would like to focus on. You will want to put this situation into context, meaning that you each should describe who is involved (e.g., you and your students, parents, and beyond) and what are the surrounding factors that play into this (e.g., what grade level and content do you each teach, what population of students do you work with). You will also pose a research question (and sub-questions) that you will investigate. You may change your research question as you move forward in a project, but it is always helpful to have a specific question that is guiding your study.

What We Know

People have been wrestling with how to build and grow equitable learning communities for a long time. Depending on the problems you and your team want to investigate, other colleagues may have conducted research that can help guide your work. Thus, another phase of action research could be a version of a literature review in which you determine what other people have learned before you begin your work. Your sources may be websites, books, interviews with experts, podcasts, or other informational texts. You can also reach out to local scholars who can help you think about the ideas driving your work.

A Plan of Action and Examination

Once you decide on your problem, you and your team can create a plan to conduct your investigation and decide on the resources you will use to gather evidence. Of course, your plans may change as your work progresses, but having a good sense for the data you want to collect and when you want to collect them are essential for your team. To help with the plan design, here are some guiding questions to consider for different categories of the work.

Overview

- What is your time frame? Is this a onetime lesson or do you anticipate several cycles of work?
- Have you done a preliminary study?
- What problem does your examination address? Is it a problem in your own practice? Or is it a problem with your students or with your administrators? Who owns the problem?
- What (initial) action will you take? What do you hope to accomplish?
- List your research questions as they appear at this time. (Questions will be revised or refocused during your examination.)

Methods

- For this research, will you gather data on your normal educational practice and on changes in curriculum, instruction, and assessment that you could make in your role according to your own professional judgment?

- List the kinds of data you plan to collect (e.g., fieldnotes, taped interviews, writing samples).
- How is this plan different from the way you normally document your practice? Consider two or three alternative ways you could gather data for this project. What are the ethical implications of choosing your preferred method?
- At this time in your research, what do you aim to understand? What do you aim to change?

Relationships

- Describe the individuals, groups, or communities you expect will be touched by your project. List their roles (student, parent, resource teacher, and so forth).
- Analyze the power relations in this group. Which people (e.g., students, parents) do you have some power over? Which people (e.g., principals, professors) have some power over you?
- What shared understandings do you have with these people? Do you have personal bonds or professional commitments? Will your research strengthen this trust or perhaps abuse it?
- Will your study attempt to read and interpret the experience of people who differ from you in race, class, gender, ethnicity, sexual orientation, or other cultural dimensions? How have you prepared yourself to share the perspective of the other (coursework, experiences, other sources of insight)?

Outcomes

- Describe the possible benefits of your research—to students, teachers, or other participants, to society or to the community.
- Describe any risks to participants. What steps are you taking to minimize risks?
- Describe how you will obtain informed consent. Do you need permission from students, parents, or both? How will you work with any students who refuse to be interviewed or to allow their materials to be quoted?

PRESENTING THE WORK TO OTHERS

Sharing your ideas about teaching and evidence of learning (from the perspective of students, teachers, and administrators) is important. There may be multiple times during your collective work that you choose to share out with various communities, including local leaders and families, colleagues in your district or across the state, and policy makers at local, state, or national levels. In addition to sharing ideas with individuals, I encourage you to present your work at local and national conferences (such as the annual meeting of the National Science Teaching Association, the NSTA) and write articles for colleagues in NSTA journals, such as *The Science Teacher*. If you are interested in presenting your work to various communities, here are some thoughts and questions to guide the work:

1. Will you record student writing, oral histories, or other documents that may be considered someone's intellectual property? How have you arranged with colleagues or students for credit in your presentation?

2. If your presentation or writing is collaborative, how are you negotiating authorship and ownership? University researchers, colleagues, students, and parents may interpret their stake in the research in quite different ways. For example, who is allowed to use the videotape of a classroom, the dialogue journal between teachers, and the transcription of a talk by teachers and students?

3. Who is responsible for what is said in the presentation? Will other stakeholders (colleagues, administrators, supervisors) review your presentation in draft form? Which participants (students, colleagues) should read your writing and ideas before presenting them to the public?

4. You will inevitably gather more data than you need. Consider why you choose some data to report to a wider audience and why some are left in your files (on what basis do you select?).

5. How will your presentation recognize the perspectives of participants who disagree with some of your interpretations? For example, you may revise your views, quote their objections and explain why you maintain your original view, or invite them to state alternative views in an appendix.

6. Have you decided on anonymity or on full acknowledgment of other participants in your presentation? Perhaps you will identify teachers but use

pseudonyms for students. If you began your study with a blanket consent form, have you now requested consent to publish specific material from specific people?

Taken together, these phases—along with other steps you and your team decide to enact—can help you publicize your wonderful work of disrupting epistemic injustice and reimagining classroom communities.

ONWARD

In conclusion, I want to thank you for engaging with the ideas. Disrupting epistemic injustice and reimagining communities in our schools and classrooms is complex, challenging, and compelling work. However, this work is crucially important for us to enact so that we can transform spaces of learning for students. While this book can provide a catalyst for conversations and action, reading and talking about the ideas is only the beginning. You can start to shift what happens in your classroom and school as early as tomorrow by taking immediate and long-term actions to change learning opportunities. You can consider the words you use to place value on students' ideas and experiences, and you can work with students to create science and teaching norms together. Working with colleagues, you can collectively help each other learn, try out, and create amazing opportunities for students.

While teaching can sometimes feel like an isolating profession, I hope that this book reminds you that you are not alone in your work. You are part of a growing community of colleagues across the United States and the world who are working together to disrupt epistemic injustice and reimagine classrooms and schools. Your words and actions, your evidence of success, and your stories will help shift conversations and policies in schools. You will inspire parents, community members, and policy makers to see that equitable classrooms and schools help students thrive. Most importantly, you will show students that you care deeply about their ideas, their experiences, and their importance as people. Thank you for traveling on the journey of this book together. I look forward to learning with and from you as we aim to reimagine classrooms and schools. I am proud of your work, I am glad to call you a colleague, and I hope you stay in touch.

NOTES

Introduction

1. Todd Campbell, Christina Schwarz, and Mark Windschitl, "What we call misconceptions may be necessary stepping-stones toward making sense of the world," Science and Children 53, no. 7 (2016): 69–74; Luis C. Moll et al., "Funds of knowledge for teaching: Using a qualitative approach to connect homes and classrooms," Theory into Practice 31, no. 2 (1992): 132–41.
2. Beth Warren et al., "Rethinking diversity in learning science: The logic of everyday sensemaking," Journal of Research in Science Teaching 38, no. 5 (2001): 529–52, doi:10.1002/tea.1017.
3. Jessica Thompson et al., "Culturally and linguistically sustaining approaches to Ambitious Science Teaching pedagogies," in Preparing Science Teachers through Practice-Based Teacher Education, ed. David Stroupe, Karen Hammerness, and Scott McDonald (Cambridge, MA: Harvard Education Press, 2020), 45–62.
4. Miranda Fricker, Epistemic Injustice: Power and the ethics of knowing (New York: Oxford University Press, 2007).
5. Ian James Kidd et al., "Introduction to the Routledge Handbook of Epistemic Injustice," in Routledge Handbook of Epistemic Injustice, ed. Ian James Kidd, José Medina, and Gaile Pohlhaus Jr. (New York: Routledge, 2017), 1.

Chapter 1

1. Douglas Medin and Megan, Who's Asking?: Native science, Western science, and science education (Cambridge, MA: MIT Press, 2014).
2. Vincent Basile and Enrique López, "And still I see no changes: Enduring views of students of color in science and mathematics education policy reports," Science Education 99 (2015): 519–48.
3. Gale Seiler, "New metaphors about culture: Implications for research in science teacher preparation," Journal of Research in Science Teaching 50, no 1 (2013): 104–21.
4. Christopher Wright, "Constructing a collaborative critique-learning environment for exploring science through improvisational performance," Urban Education 54, no. 9 (2019): 1319–48.

5. Miranda Fricker, *Epistemic Injustice: Power and the ethics of knowing* (New York: Oxford University Press, 2007); Kristie Dotson, "A cautionary tale: On limiting epistemic oppression," *Frontiers: A Journal of Women's Studies* 33, no. 1 (2012): 24–47.

6. Ian James Kidd et al., "Introduction to the *Routledge Handbook of Epistemic Injustice*," in *Routledge Handbook of Epistemic Injustice*, ed. Ian James Kidd, José Medina, and Gaile Pohlhaus Jr. (New York: Routledge, 2017), 1.

7. Gaile Pohlhaus Jr., "Relational knowing and epistemic injustice: Toward a theory of willful hermeneutical ignorance," *Hypatia* 27, no. 4 (2012): 715–35.

8. Chandra Talpade Mohanty, *Feminism Without Borders: Decolonizing theory, practicing solidarity* (Durham, NC: Duke University Press, 2004).

9. Sanford Goldberg, "Social epistemology and epistemic injustice," in *Routledge Handbook of Epistemic Injustice*, ed. Ian James Kidd, José Medina, and Gaile Pohlhaus Jr. (New York: Routledge, 2017), 213–22.

10. Miranda Fricker, "Silence and institutional prejudice," in *Out from the Shadows: Analytical feminist contributions to traditional philosophy*, ed. Sharon L. Crasnow and Anita M. Superson (New York: Oxford University Press, 2012), 287–306.

11. Michael D. Burroughs and Deborah Tollefsen, "Learning to listen: Epistemic injustice and the child," *Episteme* 13, no. 3 (2016): 359–77.

12. Matthew Congdon, "What's wrong with epistemic injustice? Harm, vice, objectification, and misrecognition," in *Routledge Handbook of Epistemic Injustice*, ed. Ian James Kidd, José Medina, and Gaile Pohlhaus Jr. (New York: Routledge, 2017), 243–53.

13. José Medina, *The Epistemology of Resistance: Gender and racial oppression, epistemic injustice, and resistant imaginations* (New York: Oxford University Press, 2013).

14. Helen Longino, *Science as Social Knowledge: Values and objectivity in scientific inquiry* (Princeton, NJ: Princeton University Press, 1990), 186.

15. Sanford Goldberg, "Social epistemology and epistemic injustice," in *Routledge Handbook of Epistemic Injustice*, ed. Ian James Kidd, José Medina, and Gaile Pohlhaus Jr. (New York: Routledge, 2017), 213–22.

16. *Ira C. Lupu, David Masci, and Robert W. Tuttle, Religion in the Public Schools* (Washington, DC: Pew Research Center, 2019), https://www.pewforum.org/2019/10/03/religion-in-the-public-schools-2019-update/.

17. Franziska Dübgen, "Epistemic injustice in practice," *Wagadu: A Journal of Transnational Women's and Gender Studies* 15 (2016): 1–10.

Chapter 2

1. Oliver Milman, "US federal department is censoring use of term 'climate change', emails reveal," *Guardian*, August 7, 2017, https://www.theguardian.com/environment/2017/aug/07/usda-climate-change-language-censorship-emails.

2. Naomi Oreskes and Erik M. Conway, *Merchants of Doubt: How a handful of scientists obscured the truth on issues from tobacco smoke to global warming* (New York: Bloomsbury Press, 2010).

3. Ebony O. McGee, *Black, Brown, and Bruised: How racialized STEM education stifles innovation* (Cambridge, MA: Harvard Education Press, 2020).
4. Sandra Harding, *Whose Science? Whose Knowledge? Thinking from women's lives* (Ithaca, NY: Cornell University Press, 1991).
5. Lynne Osman Elkin, "Rosalind Franklin and the double helix," *Physics Today* 56 no 3 (2002): 42–48.
6. Karin Knorr-Cetina, *Epistemic Cultures: How the sciences make knowledge* (Cambridge, MA: Harvard University Press, 1999).
7. Donna Haraway, "Situated knowledges: The science question in feminism and the privilege of partial perspective," *Feminist Studies* 14, no. 3 (Autumn 1988): 575–99.
8. Doug L. Medin and Megan Bang, *Who's Asking?: Native science, Western science, and science education* (Cambridge, MA: MIT Press, 2014).
9. "Tools for Ambitious Science Teaching," https://ambitiousscienceteaching.org/tools-face-to-face/.
10. Ann Rosebery, Beth Warren, and Eli Tucker-Raymond, "Developing interpretive power in science teaching," *Journal of Research in Science Teaching* 53, no. 10 (2016): 1571–600.

Chapter 3

1. Jessica Thompson et al., "C²AST (Critical and cultural approaches to Ambitious Science Teaching): From responsive teaching toward developing culturally and linguistically sustaining science teaching practices," *Science Teacher*, September/October 2021, 58–64.
2. Jessica Thompson et al., "Culturally and linguistically sustaining approaches to Ambitious Science Teaching pedagogies," in *Preparing Science Teachers Through Practice-Based Teacher Education*, ed. David Stroupe, Karen Hammerness, and Scott McDonald (Cambridge, MA: Harvard Education Press, 2020), 45–62.

Chapter 4

1. Eve Manz and Enrique Suarez, "Supporting Teachers to Negotiate Uncertainty for Science, Students, and Teaching," *Science Education* 102, no. 4 (2018): 771–95; Andrew Pickering, *The Mangle of Practice: Time, agency, and science* (Chicago: University of Chicago Press, 1995).
2. Elham Kazemi et al., "Getting inside rehearsals: Insights from teacher educators to support work on complex practice," *Journal of Teacher Education* 67, no. 1 (2016): 18–31.
3. Bruno Latour, *Science in Action: How to follow scientists and engineers through society* (Cambridge, MA: Harvard University Press, 1987).
4. Karin Knorr-Cetina, *Epistemic Cultures: How the sciences make knowledge* (Cambridge, MA: Harvard University Press, 1999), 186.
5. John Rudolph, *Scientists in the Classroom: The cold war reconstruction of American science education* (New York: Palgave, 2002).
6. Pickering, *The Mangle of Practice*, 19–20.

7. Lucy Avraamidou, "I am a young immigrant woman doing physics and on top of that I am Muslim": Identities, intersections, and negotiations," *Journal of Research in Science Teaching* 57, no. 3 (2020): 311–41.

8. Beth Warren and Ann Rosebery, "Equity in the future tense: Redefining relationships among teachers, students, and science in linguistic minority classrooms," in *Directions for Equity in Mathematics Education*, ed. Walter G. Secada et al. (New York: Cambridge University Press, 1995), 326.

9. Lynn Hankinson-Nelson, *Who Knows: From Quine to a feminist empiricism* (Philadelphia: Temple University Press, 1990).

10. Ambitious Science Teaching, "Video Gallery," Tools for Ambitious Science Teaching, June 15, 2022, https://ambitiousscienceteaching.org/video-series/; Third International Mathematics and Science Study (TIMSS) 1999 Video Study, "Home Page," June 15, 2022, http://www.timssvideo.com/.

Chapter 5

1. Megan Bang et al., "Toward more equitable learning in science: Expanding relationships among students, teachers, and science practices," in *Helping Students Make Sense of the World Using Next Generation Science and Engineering Practices*, ed. Christina V. Schwarz, Cynthia Passmore, and Brian J. Reiser (Arlington, VA: NSTA Press, 2017), 33–58.

2. *Next Generation Science Standards* (Washington, DC: Achieve, Inc., 2013).

3. Richard Duschl, "Science education in three-part harmony: Balancing conceptual, epistemic, and social learning goals," *Review of Research in Science Education* 32 (2008): 268–91.

4. Lynn Hankinson-Nelson, *Who Knows: From Quine to a feminist empiricism* (Philadelphia: Temple University Press, 1990).

5. Magdalene Lampert, "Learning teaching in, from, and for practice: What do we mean?," *Journal of Teacher Education* 61, no. 1 (2010): 21–34.

6. Sandra Harding, *Objectivity and Diversity: Another logic of scientific research* (Chicago: University of Chicago Press, 2015).

7. Helen E. Longino, *Science as Social Knowledge: Values and objectivity in scientific inquiry* (Princeton, NJ: Princeton University Press, 1990).

8. Mark Windschitl, Jessica Thompson, and Melissa Braaten, "Beyond the scientific method: Model-based inquiry as a new paradigm of preference for school science investigations," *Science Education* 92 (2008): 941–67.

9. Ron Gray, "The distinction between experimental and historical sciences as a framework for improving classroom inquiry," *Science Education* 98, no. 2 (2014): 327–41.

10. Donna Haraway, "Situated knowledges: The science question in feminism and the privilege of partial perspective," *Feminist Studies* 14, no. 3 (1988): 575–99.

11. Kathryn P. Addelson, "The man of professional wisdom," in *Discovering Reality: Feminist perspectives on epistemology, metaphysics, methodology, and philosophy of science*, ed.

Sandra Harding and Merrill B. Hintikka (Dordrecht, The Netherlands: Kluwer Academic Publishers, 1983), 165–86.

12. Sandra Harding, *Whose Science? Whose Knowledge? Thinking from women's lives* (Ithaca, NY: Cornell University Press, 1991).

13. Douglas Medin and Megan Bang, *Who's Asking?: Native science, Western science, and science education* (Cambridge, MA: MIT Press, 2014).

14. Hankinson-Nelson, *Who Knows.*

15. Windschitl et al., "Beyond the scientific method."

16. Johannes Fabian, *Out of Our Minds: Reason and madness in the exploration of Central Africa* (Berkeley: University of California Press, 2000).

17. Andrew Pickering, *The Mangle of Practice: Time, agency, and science* (Chicago: University of Chicago Press, 1995), 19–20.

18. Mark Windschitl, Jessica Thompson, and Melissa Braaten, *Ambitious Science Teaching* (Cambridge, MA: Harvard Education Press, 2018).

19. Mark Windschitl and David Stroupe, "The three-story challenge: Implications of the Next Generation Science Standards for Teacher Preparation," *Journal of Teacher Education* 68, no. 3 (2017): 251–61.

20. Mary M. Atwater, "Equity for Black Americans in pre-college science," *Science Education* 84 (2000): 154–79; Cynthia Ballenger, *Puzzling Moments, Teachable Moments* (New York: Teachers College Press, 2009).

21. Eve Manz and Enrique Suarez, "Supporting Teachers to Negotiate Uncertainty for Science, Students, and Teaching," *Science Education* 102, no. 4 (2018): 771–95.

22. Carol D. Lee, "Is October Brown Chinese? A cultural modeling activity system for underachieving students," *American Educational Research Journal* 38, no. 1 (2001): 97–141.

23. David Stroupe, "Blurring the boundaries of science: A beginning teacher and her students examine an ignored phenomenon," in *Reframing Science Teaching and Learning: Students and educators co-developing science practices in and out of school*, ed. David Stroupe (New York: Routledge, 2017): 57–72.

24. Leema Berland and Katherine McNeill, "For whom is argument and explanation a necessary distinction? A response to Osborne and Patterson," *Science Education* 96, no. 5 (2012): 808–13.

Chapter 6

1. James H. Jones, *Bad Blood: The Tuskegee syphilis experiment* (New York: Free Press, 1992); Tom Polansek, "U.S. Black farmers seek ban or product warnings for Roundup weedkiller," Reuters, August 26, 2020, https://www.reuters.com/article/bayer-lawsuit-roundup-idINL1N2FS1PP; Rebecca Skloot, *The Immortal Life of Henrietta Lacks* (New York: Crown, 2010).

2. Gloria Ladson-Billings, "From the achievement gap to the education debt: Understanding achievement in U.S. schools," *Educational Researcher* 35, no. 7 (2006): 3–13.

3. Sanford Goldberg, "Social epistemology and epistemic injustice," in *Routledge Handbook of Epistemic Injustice*, ed. Ian James Kidd, José Medina, and Gaile Pohlhaus Jr. (New York: Routledge, 2017), 213–22.

4. Kristie Dotson, "Tracking epistemic violence, tracking practices of silencing," *Hypatia* 26, no. 2 (2011): 238.

Chapter 7

1. Emily Miller et al., "Addressing the epistemic elephant in the room: Epistemic agency and the Next Generation Science Standards," *Journal of Research in Science Teaching* 55, no. 7 (2018): 1053–75.

2. Katerina Plakitsi, *Activity Theory in Formal and Informal Science Education* (Rotterdam, The Netherlands: Sense Publishers, 2013).

3. William Penuel et al., "Organizing research and development at the intersection of learning, implementation, and design," *Education Researcher* 40 (2011): 331–37.

4. Yrjö Engeström, "New forms of learning in co-configuration work," *Journal of Workplace Learning* 16, no. 1–2 (2004): 11–21; Samuel Severance et al., "Organizing for teacher agency in curricular co-design," *Journal of the Learning Sciences* 25, no. 4 (2016): 531–64.

5. Anne Edwards and Ioanna Kinti, "Working relationally at organizational boundaries: Negotiating expertise and identity," in *Activity Theory in Practice: Promoting learning across boundaries and agencies*, ed. Harry Daniels et al. (New York: Routledge, 2010), 126–39.

6. Eve Manz and Enrique Suarez, "Supporting Teachers to Negotiate Uncertainty for Science, Students, and Teaching," *Science Education* 102, no. 4 (2018): 771–95.

7. Jaana Nummijoki and Yrjö Engeström, "Towards co-configuration in home care of the elderly: Cultivating agency by designing and implementing the mobility agreement," in *Activity Theory in Practice: Promoting learning across boundaries and agencies*, ed. Harry Daniels et al. (New York: Routledge, 2010), 49–71.

Chapter 9

1. Tanya Maloney and Bree Picower, "Discussion guide," Picower-Reading group guide, http://beacon.org/Assets/PDFs/Picower-ReadingGroupGuide.pdf.

ACKNOWLEDGMENTS

THERE ARE MANY PEOPLE to thank for helping bring this book into the world. This book would not exist without the gentle requests, patience, guidance, and dedication of Jayne Fargnoli. Thanks also to Molly Grab for kind words, seeing the important details I forgot to include, and for helping to steer the writing in productive directions.

Leema Berland, Rosemary Russ, Eve Manz, Emily Miller, Sarah Michaels, Jean Moon, Rick Duschl, Heidi Carlone, Christina (Stina) Krist, Enrique (Henry) Suárez, and Déana Scipio have been fantastic thought partners over the last few years about all things epistemic. I am constantly thankful that they have pushed my thinking and suggested many ways that epistemic injustice can appear in classrooms and schools. I also am eternally grateful for the ongoing support and conversations with Mark Windschitl, Jessica Thompson, Melissa Braaten, and Hosun Kang. I also received immensely helpful guidance on writing a book that is useful for teachers and administrators from Mark Windschitl, Bryan Brown, and Doug Larkin.

I wrote this book while living in Italy on a sabbatical from Michigan State University. Thank you to Dorinda Carter Andrews for helping me navigate the sabbatical process, and for the support to learn about education in Europe. The science education team at the University of Bologna was kind, generous with time, and served as wonderful ambassadors of Italian education (and food). Thank you to Olivia Levrini, Giulia Tasquier, Francesco De Zuani, Eleonora Barelli, Martina Caramaschi, Lorenzo Miani, Sara Satanassi, and Barbara Pecori for a wonderful Italian experience! Finally, many thanks to Andres F. Maldonado de'Gàbriel for patiently helping us navigate the process of visiting Italy.

While they are featured in the book, I must specifically thank Anna Kramer and Lindsay Berk, who helped shape my understanding of teaching and learning. Anna and Lindsay helped me see what learning with students can look like in classrooms on a daily basis. I am also indebted to the time they provided to read over portions of the book, and for continually pushing my thinking in productive directions.

Finally, Erin, Emma, and Zoe helped nudge the book along, and were a wonderful audience as I talked about the book's progress. Thanks for being a wonderful family!

ABOUT THE AUTHOR

DAVID STROUPE is an associate professor of teacher education and science education, the associate director of STEM Teacher Education at the CREATE for STEM Institute, and the Director of Science and Society at State at Michigan State University. He is also an incoming associate professor of STEM education at the University of Utah. He has three overlapping areas of research interests anchored around ambitious and equitable teaching. First, he frames classrooms as science practice communities. Using lenses from Science, Technology, and Society (STS) and the History and Philosophy of Science (HPS), he examines how teachers and students disrupt epistemic injustice through the negotiation of power, knowledge, and epistemic agency. Second, he examines how beginning teachers learn from practice in and across their varied contexts. Third, he studies how teacher preparation programs can provide support and opportunities for beginning teachers to learn from practice. David has a background in biology and taught secondary life science for four years. David is the recipient of the Exemplary Research Award for the American Educational Research Association's Division K (Teaching and Teacher Education), the Early Career Research Award from the National Association for Research in Science Teaching, and "Research Worth Reading" from the National Association for Research in Science Teaching and the National Science Teacher Association.

INDEX

accountability, 29

action research, 139–145

Addelson, Kathryn, 87

administrators, 6, 21, 31
   collaboration with, 139–140
   power of, 56, 57, 82, 117
   role of, 8, 57, 107
   shared goals of teachers and, 111–121

answers, right and wrong, 39–40, 65, 81–82, 95

assessment, 8, 41, 81, 89, 132–134
   See also standardized test scores

asset maps, 61, 62

asset perspectives, 61–62

authority, 18, 28–29, 65, 82, 86–87, 104–105, 127–128

autobiography, of science learning, 61–62

Bang, Megan, 83, 87

Barton, Angela Calabrese, 83

Berk, Lindsay, 10–11, 21–30, 38–41, 46–47, 53–55, 65–68, 73–77, 90, 94–96, 111–112, 114–115, 123–138

biases, 19, 22, 38, 44, 56–57

Braaten, Melissa, 88

Brown, Bryan, 83

canonical facts, 6, 31, 66, 68, 76, 88

Christian groups, 31

claims, making, 75

classroom communities
   See also science communities
   authority in, 127–128
   codesign of, 116, 121, 124–125
   coherence in, 82, 83, 91, 92, 112, 117
   control in, 137
   culture of, 68, 73–74, 100
   empowerment to change, 20–21
   epistemic injustice in. *See* epistemic injustice
   inclusion of student voices in, 56–57
   knowledge production in, 4–5, 7, 41–42, 115
   observing, 77–78
   publicizing student thinking in, 90–91
   reflecting on, 78
   reimagining, 21–22, 47–48, 51, 56, 79, 89, 98, 99, 107–108, 115, 134–136
   rules and norms for, 124–125, 129–131
   as safe spaces, 45–46, 95, 100, 106, 124, 125, 130, 136
   science communities in, 2–6, 15
   student participation in. *See* student participation
   teaching practices in, 88–96
   tone for, 5, 15, 67–68, 74, 130

classroom examples, 9–11
   of auditing assumptions, 52–55
   of building relationships, 44–46

classroom examples, *continued*
  of codevelopment of science
    communities, 91–96
  of disrupting epistemic injustice, 21–30,
    38–41, 42–43
  of navigating complexities, 100–104
  of questioning myths about science,
    38–40
  of talk moves, 66–74
  of teaching, 42–43
classrooms. *See* classroom communities
climate crisis, 36
Cochran-Smith, Marilyn, 141
codesign, 115–117, 121
  of classrooms and schools, 116, 124–125
  principles of, 116–117
coherence, between words and actions, 82,
    83, 96, 112, 117
collaboration
  among students, 40, 42–43, 95–96
  among teachers, 135, 139–140
collective inquiry, 73, 77, 95–96, 105, 116
communication, 18, 38, 48, 57, 115, 121, 132
communities, 44, 54, 57, 65, 83
  asset perspective of, 61–62
  of learning, 73, 139–140
  marginalized, 1, 7, 21, 22, 42
  partnerships with, 114
  perpetuating injustice in, 106
  shared goals for schools and, 111–121
competition, 77
complexities, in reimagining classrooms,
    99–109
conceptual dimension, of disciplinary
    work, 84
conceptual thinking, 115–116
controversial ideas, equal time for, 30–31
conversation
  classroom, 3–5, 19, 24–29
  opportunities for, 89–90
  promotion of, 65–74

correct answers, 31–32, 81–82, 95
COVID pandemic, 31, 36
creationism, 31
credibility, 18
Crick, Francis, 37
critical consciousness, 56
critical thinking, 132
cultural knowledge, 52–53, 83
cultures, 57

deficit perspective, of students, 6–7, 9, 15
delivery pedagogy, 6–7, 9, 15, 41, 134
deregulation, 36
disciplinary work
  dimensions of, 84–85
  learning to participate in, 85
DNA research, 37
dominant groups, 17
dominant norms, 19, 20, 31
Dotson, Kristie, 106

education
  higher, 137
  purpose of, 132–133
  system, 137
education debt, 106
education researchers, 120
epistemic agency, 75–76
epistemic dimension, of disciplinary work,
    84
epistemic friction, 22, 27–28
epistemic injustice
  action research on, 141–145
  challenges in disrupting, 99–109
  confronting, 15–33
  creating conditions for, 16–17
  defined, 17–18
  disrupting, 8–9, 11–12, 21–33, 38–43,
    46, 56, 83

forms of, 18–20
importance of disrupting, 15–16
knowledge production and, 17
myth of equal opportunities and, 43–46
perpetuation of, 106
shared goals for disrupting, 111–121
talk moves that perpetuate, 69–72
epistemic resources, 28
equal opportunities, myth of, 43–46
equal time, for controversial ideas, 30–31
equity
in the future tense, 76–77
lens, 47, 134–136
in science education, 7–8
experimentation, 86, 88, 94–95

face-to-face tools, 38–39
false narratives, 31
Franklin, Rosalind, 37
Fricker, Miranda, 8, 17

goal setting, 135
grades, 55–56
See also assessment
Gray, Ron, 86
group work, 40, 95–96, 130, 133

Haraway, Donna, 38
Harding, Sandra, 86
hermeneutical injustice, 18–19
hierarchical injustice, 20
higher education, 137
home life, 129
home visits, 128
hypotheses
criteria for, 25
generating, 39–40
testing, 25–26

ideas
See also student ideas
consideration of, 105–106
equal time for controversial, 30–31
exclusion of, from science, 38
integration of, 75
off-track, 131–132
sharing, 144–145
idea spaces, 93–94
identities, 17
imposter syndrome, 134
individuality, 77, 116
information acquisition, 28
information delivery, 6–7, 9, 15, 41, 132, 134
injustice. See epistemic injustice
instructional adaptations, 54–55, 73–74, 102–104
instructions, 71
intrapersonal injustice, 19

job-related skills, 132–133
Johnson, Heather, 56

Kidd, Ian James, 8, 18
Knorr-Cetina, Karin, 73
knowledge, 17
authority over, 82
biases toward, 22
canonical, 6, 31, 66, 68, 76, 88
cultural, 52–53, 83
privileged forms of, 44, 66, 76
knowledge diversity, 106
knowledge production
in the classroom, 4–5, 7, 41–42, 115
dominant groups and, 17
epistemic injustice and, 8–9, 17, 31–32
new means of, 106
practices for, 81–98

knowledge production, *continued*
  by students, 7, 9, 15, 41–42, 76–77, 89,
    95–96, 115
Kramer, Anna, 10–11, 39, 42–47, 52–55, 57,
    65–66, 68, 73–77, 88–94, 100–104,
    111–115, 123–138

Lacks, Henrietta, 105
Lampert, Magdalene, 85
learning
  asset perspective of, 61–62
  assumption audit, 60–61
  assumptions about, 55–57
  communities of, 73, 139–140
  definition of, 60–61
  evidence of, 114
  for real world, 132–133
  student thinking as main driver of, 12
learning opportunities, 1
  codesigned, 24, 28–30
  equity in, 7, 47
  myth of equal, 43–46
  myths about science and schools that
    limit, 35–49
  outside stakeholders and, 118–120
  participatory, 64
  for reasoning through talk, 89–90
  teaching practices and, 88–96
listening, virtuous, 22, 28
lived experiences, 29, 44–46, 57, 66, 90,
    134–135
lobbyists, 36
Longino, Helen, 29
Luehmann, April, 56
Lytle, Susan, 141

Maloney, Tanya, 140
Manz, Eve, 64
marginalization, 31

marginalized communities, 1, 7, 21, 22,
    42
marginalized people
  epistemic injustice and, 18–20
  science and, 105
marginalized students
  epistemic injustice and, 20–22
  experiences of, 16–17
  knowledge production by, 31–32
  myth of equal opportunities for, 43–46
  participation by, 17, 41–42
  treatment of, 43–44
material dimension, of disciplinary work,
    84
Mawyer, Kirsten, 56
Medin, Doug, 87
memorization, 6
meritocracy, 43–44
messiness, of science, 73–74, 88, 94–95
metacognitive questions, 69
microaggressions, 16–17
misinformation, 31
Monsanto, 105
"move on" moments, 72
multiple perspectives, 30–31
myths
  about equal opportunities, 43–46
  about science, 35–41
  about teaching, 41–43

naming, of groups harmed, 22, 27
Next Generation Science Standards, 5,
    83, 114
No Child Left Behind, 118–119
norms
  dominant, 19, 20, 31
  of school, 43, 44, 65
  science, 29, 37, 38, 84, 85, 87
norm setting, 8, 65, 89, 91, 92, 124–125,
    129–131

off-track ideas, 131–132

parents, 5, 56, 65, 99, 108, 129
pedagogical complexities, 99–109
pedagogy, delivery, 6–7, 9, 15, 41
peer review, 90–91, 136
performance tasks, 133
Pickering, Andrew, 74, 88
Picower, Bree, 140
policy makers, 118–119
politics, of science, 36, 38
power
    redistributing to students, 54
    science practice and, 86–87
    sharing, 127–128
    of teachers and administrators, 56, 57,
        82, 117, 124
power structures, 16, 42, 76–77, 115, 136
professional development, 6, 12
professional learning communities,
        139–140

questions
    clarifying, 69
    encouraging, 131
    metacognitive, 69
    for participation, 69
    rhetorical, 69
    to solicit information, 69
    by students, 76, 131
    of teachers, 137–138

reasoning, 71
recitation, 6
red light/green light tool, 39
relationship building, 44–46, 123–129
restorative justice, 7
revoicing, 70

rhetorical questions, 69
right answers, 39–40, 65, 81–82, 95
Rosebery, Ann, 76–77, 83

safe spaces, 45–46, 95, 100, 106, 124, 125,
        130, 136, 140
"sage on the stage," 6, 41
scaffolding, 90, 91, 98, 133
schools
    See also classroom communities
    codesign of, 116, 121
    observing, 77–78
    outside stakeholders and, 118–120,
        132–134
    as part of society, 16–17
    reimagining, 99
    shared goals for communities and,
        111–121
school year, beginning of, 2, 129–131
science
    assumption audit, 57–58
    complexities around, 105–106
    definition of, 57
    dimensions of, 84–85
    diversity within fields of, 37–38
    exclusion from, 36–37
    fields of, 86
    as helpful or harmful, 105
    messiness of, 73–74, 88, 94–95
    myths about, 35–41
    nature of, 86
    politics and, 36, 38
    as public practice, 73, 96
    in real world, 117
    as separate from society, 36
    situating in communities and lives, 57
    unpredictability in, 64
science classrooms
    assumptions about, 51–62
    beginning of school year and, 129–131

science classrooms, *continued*
  disrupting epistemic injustice in, 21–30
  hierarchical injustice in, 20
  science practices in, 83–88
  student participation in, 2–5, 29–32,
    42–46
science communities
  in classrooms, 2–6, 15
  codevelopment of, 91–98, 115–117
  creation of, 12
  epistemic injustice and, 9
  equitable, 7–8
  ideas shaping, 30–32, 38, 44–46
  reimagining, 47–48
science education
  changing expectations for, 6–8
  equity in, 7–8
  principles of equitable, 83
  reform of, 5–6
  resources for, 6
science knowledge, 2–3, 29–32, 36
  creation of, 65–66
  as main objective, 84
  student shaping of, 30–32, 38, 41–42,
    65–66, 68, 76–77, 136
science practices, 82–88, 96–98, 107
  contextual circumstances for, 86–87
  definition of, 84
  dimensions of disciplinary work, 84–85
  over time, 87–88
  participation in disciplinary work, 85
  public or private, 87
  themes about, from science studies,
    85–88
scientific method, 37, 86, 88
scientists
  assumptions about, 35–36
  opportunities to become, 36–37, 76
  professional, 119–120
Scipio, Deana, 56
self-worth, 129

sensemaking, 7, 83
shared goals, 111–121
signals, 70
small group models, 39
social dimension, of disciplinary work, 84
social inequities, 16
social justice, 7
social norms, 16
society, science as separate from, 36
stakeholders, 118–120, 132–134
standardized test scores, 114, 119, 132–134
sticky notes, 39
student ideas
  acknowledging, 15
  assigning value to, 65, 68, 76
  dismissal of, 18
  elevating, 126–127
  off-track, 131–132
  publicizing, 90–91
  pushing or pulling, 72
  as resources, 41–42, 90
  safe spaces for, 95, 126
  shaping science communities, 30–32,
    38, 42–46, 68, 76, 136
  sharing, 3–5, 126, 127, 130
  teachers' responses to, 2–5, 12, 68, 76,
    81–82, 102–107, 135, 136
student learning. *See* learning
student outcomes, 114
student participation, 2–5, 29–30, 41–43,
    82, 89, 92–93
  acknowledging, 127
  correct answers and, 31–32
  designing for, 117
  encouraging, 126–127
  marginalized students and, 17, 41–42
  talk moves and, 64–74
students
  as active knowledge producers, 7, 9, 15
  assessment of, 8, 41, 81, 89, 132–134
  asset perspective of, 61–62

assumptions about, 51–62
building relationships with, 44–46, 57, 123–129
codevelopment of science communities by, 91–98
collaboration among, 40, 42–43, 95–96
communities of, 54, 57
cultures of, 57
deficit views of, 6–7, 9, 15
empowerment of, 104, 125–127, 134
epistemic agency by, 75–76
getting to know your, 135
goals of, 135
knowledge production by, 31–32, 76–77, 89, 95–96, 115
learning from, 52–55
lived experiences of, 29, 44–46, 57, 90, 134–135
marginalized. *See* marginalized students
myth of equal opportunities for all, 43–46
myths that limit opportunities for, 35–49
outside of class and school, 44–45, 128–129
sensemaking by, 83
talk moves by, 74–77, 81
treatment of, 8–9, 48
use of authority by, 28–29
validating, 124, 131
Suárez, Enrique, 64
summarizing, 71
summary table, 39

tagging on, 71
talk moves, 3, 39–40, 63–79, 81–82
  activities for, 77–78
  opportunities for, 89–90
  for participatory opportunities, 69–72

purposeful, 65–74
by students, 74–77, 89–90
that perpetuate epistemic injustice, 69–72
tangential talk, 72
teacher preparation programs, 118–119
teachers
  authority of, 65, 82, 104–105
  biases of, 22, 44, 56–57
  challenges for, 137–138
  codevelopment of science communities by, 91–98
  collaboration among, 135, 139–140
  information delivery by, 6–7, 9, 15, 41, 134
  internal image of, 41
  perpetuating injustice, 106
  power of, 8, 15, 18, 22, 42, 56, 117, 124, 127–128
  professional development for, 6, 12
  questions of, 137–138
  responses by, to student ideas, 2–5, 105–107
  responsibility of, 56
  role of, 1, 15, 104–105, 107, 132, 134, 136
  salaries of, 133
  scaffolding by, 91, 98
  shared goals of administrators and, 111–121
  support and retention of, 118–119
  talk moves by, 3, 39–40, 65–74, 77–78, 81–82
  tool design by, 97–98
  trust building by, 29
  White, 19, 56, 136
  work load for, 137–138
teaching
  asset perspective of, 61–62
  assumption audit, 59–60
  assumptions about, 55–57, 64
  challenges of, 137–138

teaching, *continued*
    changing nature of, 132
    definition of, 59
    myths about, 41–43
    navigating uncertainty in, 63, 64
    professionalization of, 119
    reimagining, 47–48
teaching practices, 82–83, 88–98
teamwork, 132
tensions, in reimagining classrooms, 99–109
testimonial injustice, 18
testimony, 18
tests, 132–134
Thompson, Jessica, 56, 88
trust, 73
trust building, 29, 74, 123–129
Tuskegee experiment, 105

uncertainty, navigating, 63, 64, 117

virtuous listening, 22, 28

Warren, Beth, 76–77, 83
Watson, James, 37
White men, scientific exclusion and, 19, 37, 76, 105
White teachers, 19, 56, 136
whole class discussions, 130
whole class model, 39
Wilkins, Maurice, 37
Windschitl, Mark, 88, 89
wrong answers, 39–40, 65, 95